Between Two Worlds

An Armenian-American Woman's Journey Home

Jemela S. Macer, Ph.D.

Cover design by Jennifer Leigh Selig
Map of Turkey by BMR Williams

EMPRESS
PUBLICATIONS
WWW.EMPRESSPUBLICATIONS.COM

Author's Note

This is a work of creative nonfiction. In some places, conversations or events that have not been remembered in their entirety have been improvised or combined to capture the spirit of the experience. In some instances, composite characters have been created, and some names changed to protect the privacy of individuals.

All the thoughts and feelings explored here are mine and mine alone, born of my particular psychological makeup and ways of experiencing life. Those raised in the same home or the same culture and under similar circumstances may well remember or view these experiences differently. I have done my best to stay as close to my emotional truth as possible in recounting events and experiences.

Jemela S. Macer, Ph.D.
La Cañada, California
May, 2023

For

Jemela Mahsereghian,
the grandmother I never knew,
whose spirit guided me every step of the way,

and for **Alicia,** my daughter, who,
with her children and her children's children,
will carry on the journey.

Table of Contents

If you look deeply into the palm of your hand, you will see your
parents and all generations of your ancestors.
All of them are alive at this moment. Each is present in your body.
You are the continuation of each of these people.

~Thích Nhất Hạnh

The Dream of the Baby

I sit alone in what feels like a wooden Adirondack chair, my spine slightly tilted backward, my legs raised over an extended footstool. Suddenly, someone I cannot see from my left side hands me a baby, not a newborn but still a wee baby. She's quiet and stares up as if watching something. A tight, once-white blanket swaddles her; a dirtied white bonnet rests upon her head. Like a misty chiaroscuro cloud, a dark film surrounds her, obscuring her features.

I reach my arms out involuntarily yet hesitantly toward her. My head moves from side to side, looking for someone, asking silently, "Why are you giving this baby to me? What am I supposed to do with this baby? This baby doesn't belong to me."

Yet I accept her, holding her far from me, my arms outstretched. I am befuddled and have no clue what to do with her. I look around again to see whose baby it is, to give it back, but I see no one. I have the sense that I've never held a baby before.

I gradually bring her closer to my body, her little feet against my chest, her head cupped in my hand. The black mist begins to dissolve, to pull away, revealing her dark brown eyes and olive skin. I look into those eyes and make contact with her. I bring her closer. I hug her and hold her and coo at her. Gradually she begins to smile back at me and make little gurgling sounds.

She becomes an actual breathing entity, and I begin to embrace her as my own.

Though I have no idea how much time has passed, I feel love and warmth for this baby. "I want to keep this baby," I think, and I grasp her more tightly to my breast.

When I wake from the dream, I know immediately that the baby represents these writings, this book. Some unseen force gave her to me. I held her at bay for a long time and couldn't see what she looked like or what I was supposed to do with her. She was indeed shrouded in a hazy mist.

She wasn't given to me clean and pristine but with dirtied clothes and shrouded in darkness, like an orphan born of genocide and trauma. At first, she was silent, but gradually, as I held her and interacted with her, she warmed up. Expressions crossed her face, and she uttered some of who she was, though I didn't always understand her messages. She began to find her voice as I began to find mine, and we entered into conversation.

She came to me from my left side, traditionally signifying the feminine, the receptive, and the mother. Perhaps she arrived from my grandmother and my female ancestors as a gift to be seen, held, and cared for. Like my Armenian identity.

She has become mine, and I am learning to love and treasure her.

I now share her with you.

Preface

For as long as I can remember, I have wanted to write about family. I wasn't sure what I wanted to say, but the call lived within me from an early age.

In the summer of 2015, based upon what I would later understand as a spiritual nudge and a desire to understand more about the lives of my four deceased Armenian grandparents, I embarked upon a journey to what was once ancient Western Armenia, now a part of modern-day Turkey. During that trip, sixteen strangers and I, all Armenians from various parts of the Armenian diaspora, visited the birthplaces and ancestral homes of our parents and grandparents.

Growing up, I heard next to nothing about the lives of my grandparents in the "old country" or their experiences immigrating to Ellis Island in the early years of the twentieth century. What I found in visiting that "old country" shook my soul in unforeseen ways. I visited their places of birth as I had hoped to. But what I discovered there, amidst the ruins and remnants of the Armenian culture, was a portal into the horrors of the 1915 Armenian Genocide, a genocide about which I had read much but heard nothing from my family members who had experienced it, or their children—my parents.

Peering through that portal into the devastation of the genocide, I wondered about the possible transgenerational effects of trauma that had lain dormant for decades within me, my parents, and my grandparents. How might anxieties, traumas, and even belief structures unknowingly pass on from generation to generation? How much of my struggle with lifelong mild depression and my inner hunger for something indefinable may have resulted from my parents' and grand-parents' undigested, unhealed experiences?

Most importantly, I sought to explore the question which had troubled me from the beginning: What does healing look like? How do we heal from traumas passed down from one generation to another and prevent the passing of these traumas onto our children and our children's children?

After the inner tumult that followed my 2015 tour to ancient Armenia, which I began to refer to as "The Genocide Tour," the call to explore my family roots and their impact on my present life burned more deeply within me.

In late 2016, a flyer appeared in my inbox from Pacifica Graduate Institute in Santa Barbara, California, devoted to the study of depth psychology and the works of C.G. Jung. The flyer was an invitation to join a memoir class, "Writing Down the Soul." I opened and re-opened that flyer for over a year. Finally, in the early spring of 2018, at the age of 62, I pushed "send" on the registration form.

That first memoir course became a second, and then a third, a fourth, a fifth, and finally a sixth. This memoir results from those five years of writing, week after week, month after month, word after word.

When the pandemic struck in March 2020, like most of us, I was locked within my world.

My writing took an unexpected turn, becoming an outlet for pent-up thoughts and feelings about every aspect of our human experience. I contemplated the nature of trauma, the etiology of depression, and the impact of war and genocide on families and cultures. This memoir includes writings and journal entries from that unprecedented time

A connecting cultural and spiritual thread of Family and Identity weaves its way throughout the chapters of this memoir. Many were, however, written as separate vignettes, windows into moments of time, neither chronological nor necessarily connected by time and place. As a result, I've organized the memoir into four sections.

"Identity" discusses my early life and growing into adulthood in Southern California as an Armenian-American, including my work as a cross-cultural clinical psychologist. These glimpses are into my life before the Genocide Tour.

"The Genocide Tour" describes my 2015 trip to Turkey on the 100th anniversary of the Armenian Genocide and my reflections on that trip. That experience opened up within me a deeper exploration and understanding of my identity as a second-generation Armenian-American.

"Thoughts on Culture and Identity During a Global Pandemic" includes journal entries and other writings from that time, especially as they relate to my experience of being an Armenian in Southern California and the grandchild of genocide survivors.

Finally, **"Finding the Mandorla"** explores how my understanding of myself as an Armenian and an American came to intersect and integrate within me in part because of this writing process.

For those of you who are non-Armenians, or who know little about the Armenian culture, I hope that you come to appreciate something of this culture from which I spring and what it means to be the grandchild of genocide survivors. If you are Armenian, I hope you'll find something of yourself and your families' experiences in these pages and ponder anew what it means to be an Armenian, with our long history and rich cultural legacy. Finally, I hope a portal may be opened within you, the reader, into your psyche and soul, inspiring similar questions and reflections upon your life as it relates to your ancestral heritage.

Prologue

*All good stories are mandorlas. Through the miracle of the story, (they)
demonstrate that opposites overlap and are finally the same. . . . As time
passes, the greater the overlap, the greater and more complete the healing.
The mandorla binds together that which was torn apart and made
unwhole—unholy.*

~Robert Johnson

I pick up a black and brown, unevenly shaped stone, craters pock-
marking its surface. It's one from the myriad of rocks my husband
Jim has laid out on our living room table—black meteorites, small
beige pebbles from a rushing stream, a polished, blue lapis in the shape
of an eagle, and an orange citrine carved into the form of a serpent.
These stones have been gathered and blessed by mountain shamans
from the Andes in Peru and from Jim's travels throughout the world.

I blow three long, hard breaths into the cratered stone. I blow the
tightness in my stomach, the heaviness in my heart, and the fear in my
chest into the stone. Jim asks that the stone absorb whatever within
me needs healing. With his right hand, he unwinds my third chakra
counterclockwise and asks me to lie down on the massage table. He
places the stone over the chakra, located at my solar plexus, and walks
around the table, shaking his small Peruvian rattle. I close my eyes and
breathe gently and deeply in through my nose and out through my
mouth.

In his mind, Jim silently journeys down through my third chakra, deep into the earth, into what the shamans call the "lower world." There he finds the four caves that South American healers believe hold our secrets: the Cave of Wounds, the Cave of Contracts, the Cave of Grace, and the Cave of Gifts.

In his mind's eye, he enters the Cave of Wounds and pauses briefly. He sees rows of terrified, dark-haired men lined up against a wall in a town square, waiting to be executed. Toward the back corner of the cave, long lines of haggard women and children clutch each other as they are pushed into the stifling desert by uniformed soldiers.

Later, when he describes this to me, I experience a shock of recognition. A heavy dark blanket of dread chills my heart. I have read of these experiences in the many books I have devoured on the Armenian Genocide.

From the Cave of Wounds, he moves quickly into the Cave of Contracts. He looks around the stark grey cave, searching for some indication of a contract I might have brought with me into this life related to the wounding he witnessed in the Cave of Wounds. There, written largely in white paint on the side of a crumbling wall, he sees "Life is not always safe. Beware."

I understand this immediately, having experienced it in my bones.

Next, he enters the Cave of Grace, where he meets an aspect of my healed Self, an aspect that may have fled due to trauma or abuse, but has remained whole and harmonious in this lower world. A young woman dressed in traditional Armenian clothing stands tall, her arms held upward as if ready to dance, her black braids reaching almost to her waist. Silver coins stretch across the forehead of her colorful head-dress, and a long wine-red velvet tunic embroidered with gold thread lies atop her long, flowing cream-white dress. She smiles broadly. I delight in her vision when Jim describes it and can easily imagine her, but she feels Other and not a part of me at all.

In the final cave, the Cave of Gifts, Jim sees a single pair of Nike running shoes in the center. I wonder about this particular gift.

"Would you like to enter the caves yourself and converse with any of their occupants?" he asks.

"Yes," I answer.

This time, he guides me down into the lower world. I close my eyes and move deep into the belly of the earth, through the gnarled roots of ancient trees, to a layer of soft brown soil. It gives way to molten rock, and, finally, to a gently flowing river. I lie in the river, and it carries me downstream until I reach the entrance to the section of the lower world that houses the caves. I ask the gatekeeper if I may enter the caves. He waves me in.

I choose to enter the Cave of Gifts first. "Why are you here?" I ask the Nikes. "What purpose do you serve?"

"We are here to provide stamina and support for you as you walk this journey," they respond.

Hmm, what's that supposed to mean? What journey?

Jim asks if I am ready to receive the gift of the Nikes. I don't completely understand what this means, but I say yes, and he blows them into my second chakra, below my navel, the chakra of energy and passion, fight or flight. He then gently closes the chakra, sealing it clockwise with his hand.

The beautiful Armenian woman beckons me in as I enter the Cave of Grace.

"Who are you, and why are you here?" I ask.

"I am the personification of your Armenian self," she replies.

Jim asks her if she is ready to integrate into my being. She hesitates. Perhaps she wonders if she will be welcomed, honored, and cherished as she deserves. She stares at me and slowly shakes her head no. She is choosing to remain safe in the lower world. This doesn't surprise me. The woman looks foreign to me, and while I find her fascinating, I feel no resonance with her.

I am too frightened to enter the Cave of Wounds, not interested in returning to what I know to be the Armenian Genocide. I understand the contract well from the Cave of Contracts, that life can be unsafe, to beware. I choose not to enter that cave, either.

Now it's time to return to the upper world. A big black bull appears to accompany me down the river and up through the earth and back to where I lay on the massage table. I ask the bull why he has appeared. "To give you strength and stability and hold you close to the earth," he responds.

I am grateful for his solid presence as he travels back with me. Jim blows the image of the bull into my root chakra, the chakra of survival, which spans the base of my spine and the pelvic region,

When I started this excavation of my Armenian cultural heritage, I had no idea it would become nothing less than a retrieval of a lost, cutoff part of my soul. The ritual of soul retrieval, commonly practiced among shamans in indigenous cultures, seeks to reunite lost soul pieces to their original whole. Soul pieces flee for many reasons: trauma, survival, shame, protection, and rejection. During the act of soul retrieval, the healer reaches deep into the lower world to invite lost soul parts to return to the larger soul from whence they fled. If the errant part is ready to reunite with its soul, it can be blown back into the chakras and the energetic field, creating wholeness. If not, it stays behind in the lower world until it is ready to return.

Like Hermes, the winged Greek god and child of Zeus, who ferried messages between the earthly world and the other beyond the veil, I have lived between worlds—between the modern American of my California upbringing and the ancient Armenian of my ancestors, in the energetic space between two individuals sitting opposite each other in the therapy room, and between the material world and the numinous in my spiritual life.

Like Hermes, we all form bridges between the past and the present, between our ancestors, many generations removed and our children yet to be borne, and between cultures left behind in the old world and the newer cultures into which we assimilate. We bridge the space between us as individuals and, for those who believe, between this material world and the numinous world of spirit surrounding us. Sometimes, pieces of those worlds may be too painful to inhabit, so we send them deep into the unconscious to come forth at a later date, if ever.

How do we live in both worlds, the ancient and the modern, the earthly and the numinous? How do we live in that precious space where the two worlds intersect? And how do we bring back soul pieces that may have fled a hundred years ago from a different generation?

This is my story of bridging worlds and finding those lost soul pieces. I seek to find that almond-shaped mandorla formed in the center where two circles overlap. I strive to live within that mandorla, that holy place between worlds that encompasses them both.

SECTION ONE

Identity

From my earliest years, I experienced a yearning for something larger and deeper than my comfortable life in Southern California. I searched, traveling the world from Europe to Asia to South America, looking to fulfill that inner longing.

As a clinical psychologist, I began to work in the Southern California city which had become home to the largest diaspora of Armenians outside Armenia. There, through my Armenian clients and the city itself, I came to know my ancestral heritage in a way I had never experienced. These chapters weave together the themes of family, identity formation, and the search for an inner sense of home.

Chapter 1

Yearning

I stand in diapers, a small, round girl of 18 months, on the plush beige carpet of my father's study, staring at the back of his mane of wavy, chestnut hair. My father sits silently in his brown Naugahyde swivel chair, leaning intently over the mahogany desk with its forest green ink blotter. Smoke wafts up from the pipe in the ashtray. I breathe in the beloved aroma. My father either purposely ignores me or is unaware of my presence.

No one else is in the room. I continue to stare, willing him to turn around, wanting something from him but not knowing what. It's one of my earliest memories.

The adult in me asks the little girl what she wants. "Just to be with him," she responds. "Just to be in his presence." I crave his attention as I crave the attention of almost everyone else in my family. But they are busy.

My family elicited the envy of many in the extended Armenian community of our Los Angeles area. A respected physician father, a doting and vivacious wife and mother, a Spanish home in a middle-class community surrounded by ochre hills, canyons to hike in, and four charming, well-behaved children. A white Jensen Interceptor 3 sedan sat at the base of the driveway which curled up to the kitchen door from the street. A rolling green lawn stretched the length of the front of the house, sloping upwards towards the road.

As a child, I'd scramble up the green hill and roll down it with the Christensen kids, who lived next door. I played baseball there with my two older brothers and the neighborhood children.

My father's sister, my favorite Aunty Gladys, lived a mile away. Around her glass kitchen table, I learned to make baklava and to roll out perfect dough for apple pie. We drank endless Diet Cokes and ate tuna fish sandwiches. I'd steal Snickers bars and Milky Ways from her secret candy drawer as she pretended not to notice. On Sundays, Aunty Gladys, Uncle Henry, and my cousin Carol came over to barbecue lamb or shish kebab. Dad's Aunty Vic and Uncle Mike and their kids Hank and John came too. Everyone lived close by in our Altadena neighborhood.

Hollywood, with its Grauman's Chinese Theatre, the Hollywood Wax Museum, and the star-strewn sidewalk of Hollywood Boulevard, existed a mere 20-minute drive away. Once, when I was about twelve, I ran into Robert Redford and Paul Newman outside the pawnshop on Colorado Boulevard in Pasadena as they were filming *The Sting*. On another occasion, Barbra Streisand sat behind me at the local movie theatre.

An orchard of avocado, lemon, olive, fig, apricot, orange, and tangerine trees lined the backyard, bordered by rose gardens. Every Saturday morning in the fall, I'd rake the leaves fallen from the fruit trees out from under the roses as part of my weekly chores. In December, when the tangerines ripened, my brother Jim and I would climb high into the tree's upper branches to harvest the biggest orbs, stopping to eat as many tangerines as we could stomach on the way up.

As a little girl, I'd often climb into the thick branches of the avocado tree, its ancient limbs supporting me. I spent much time sitting alone in the tree's branches, thinking and wondering.

In all outward respects, I had an idyllic childhood, the epitome of the American dream that my immigrant grandparents and their first-generation children had worked so hard to attain. I had unending access to plentiful, home-cooked food, a room of my own, an acre of land to play on, and lots of friends to play with. We had money to buy whatever we needed.

But something within me felt missing, an emptiness that I could never place, an inner loneliness amidst the plenty. I desired, above all, a connection to something I couldn't name, couldn't see, and couldn't hear. Was it a person, the Divine, or myself?

I would spend a lifetime trying to unearth that lack and that hole, trying to make it whole.

Chapter 2

The Visitations

66 An old woman I don't know is talking to me in a language I don't understand. She's saying something about a book. She wants you to write a book. She seems very, very adamant. Are you writing a book?"

I had been wolfing down tortilla chips and salsa at Mijares, our local Mexican hangout, when Raven, my officemate, suddenly held her hand up to my face as if to say "Stop" and whispered these sentences into my ear. I jolted to attention, the blood draining from my face.

"Do you know who she is? Are you writing a book?" Raven asked. I said no, I wasn't writing a book, and no, I didn't know who she was. But in my heart, I knew exactly who she was: my Grandmother Jemela, who had come to me in a vision years earlier.

I had only grudgingly agreed to meet my two officemates and their husbands for a Friday night margarita at Mijares. Among my friends and family, I'm known for a certain curmudgeonliness on Friday nights, weary from a week's listening to the world's woes and wanting nothing more than to tuck myself into bed with a good, thick book. To make matters worse, I didn't know this new officemate Raven too well and was, admittedly, more than a little intimidated by her long mane of black hair, her many sojourns to Tibet and Nepal and Europe to teach Tibetan shamanism, and a certain knowing look in her intense black eyes that gave off an air of unapproachable self-confidence. I sometimes found myself shying away from her in our office hallways between sessions and sneaking into our bathroom when her office door was open.

And now here I was, sitting next to her at the table this Friday night. As I'd dragged myself into the restaurant earlier, I had run into her husband, Tomas, an anthropology professor at a local university. I indicated to him that I was none too happy to be there. He had grinned sweetly and responded, "What you resist persists, Jemela." Shit, I thought. Now she whispered into my ear, saying that someone in an accented voice told her I should write a book.

In my mind, I was back at the North Rim of the Grand Canyon on a summer day in August 2011, several years earlier. My husband Jim and I had stopped at the North Rim on our way home from dropping our daughter Alicia off for her first year of college at UT Austin. We'd driven twenty-four hours through West Texas's interminably dull, hot flatlands. When we arrived at the isolated North Rim, the crisp mountain air and bright blue skies provided a welcome respite from the summer's heat wave ravaging Texas.

Jim had once dreamed of honeymooning in one of Arizona's little cabins overlooking the North Rim. I had other ideas: Tahiti maybe, Santorini perhaps, or best yet, Katmandu. But the Grand Canyon? In Arizona? No way. There was no way this native Californian was going to Arizona for her honeymoon. So we didn't go to the Grand Canyon. Still, in what was to become a theme in our marriage, we compromised with Akumal, Mexico, near enough to home for Jim's comfort level and just exotic enough to satisfy my yearning for the far-flung.

Twenty-five years later, I had made a reservation to spend our twenty-fifth wedding anniversary in one of those little cabins. After our many years together, I had mellowed and come to join Jim in his appreciation of the epic wonders of the Grand Canyon.

That August morning, we drove around the park and stopped at a vast, shimmering green meadow stretching along the main road to the lodge at the rim. The smell of morning dew permeated the air. We walked toward a clump of low trees and monolithic, gray rocks burrowed into the hill abutting the meadow. I scrambled atop the giant, flattest boulder I could find. It was a warm, robin's egg blue day; the air was still, and no one was around.

Jim, a physician-turned-energy practitioner, asked if I wanted to take a shamanic journey. I said, "Sure," and laid my head against the cold stone, stretching my legs as far as they could go.

"Begin to breathe in through your nose and out through your mouth," he began, and I breathed in and out slowly until my limbs became jelly against the cold stone. "See a large tree in front of you," he continued, leading me on an inner journey up through the tree's branches into the endless blue sky. Soon the tree turned into a wooden ladder stretching upward into what seemed like infinity. I began to climb the ladder. I passed the mythical land of the stone people described to us by the indigenous shamans of the Andes, and then the land of the plant people. Soon I peered into the land of the animals, watching deer and gazelle skitter across the green grass and monkeys fly from trees, giant snakes crawling beneath them on the wet soil. But I was not called to stop there. I kept climbing and arrived in the fourth world, where humans go after death, according to the Quechua healers of the high Andes with whom Jim had been working for several years.

"Look around, see who awaits you." Jim's voice sounded far away. "Who do you see?"

I was in a deep trance and looked around to see who might greet me. There before me, I noticed my paternal grandmother. I recognized her from our old, frayed black-and-white photographs: prominent nose, pockmarked face, stocky body in a floral shirtwaist dress, sensible black leather shoes, and piercing eyes.

She stared directly at me. Her intense gaze frightened me.

"Heal me," she said.

"Heal me," she repeated.

"Live the life I could not live."

I was taken aback. I had never before had an encounter with my paternal grandmother, nor had I ever dreamed of her or hardly even thought of her.

I had come into this world a year after my grandmother died suddenly of ovarian cancer and was named after her, Jemela. Who names a little American girl Jemela in the 1950s? On the advice of their obstetrician, and as a precaution, my parents gave me the middle name "Sue" just in case I couldn't handle the weird foreign first name. As it turned out, I dealt with the odd foreign name just fine. Others in my life didn't handle it quite as well, though, and took to calling me "Sue" at an early age.

Growing up, I rarely remembered Grandmother Jemela's name mentioned, so terrible was the memory of her early, tragic death, or so I imagined. I knew almost nothing about her because, in my family, we told no stories. We lived life in the frenetic present and the projected future. The past seemed not to exist. For all I knew, my family history began in 1912 when my grandmother gave birth to my father in New York City.

I was the fourth-born and youngest in my Armenian-American family. Though my parents were full-blooded Armenians and the children of poor immigrants, they raised us as Americans rather than Armenians. Unlike most Armenian families who attended Armenian churches and Armenian schools and whose surnames ended in "ian," I attended the local Presbyterian church, walked to the public elementary school down the block, and had the surname "Macer." Dad had shortened his last name while in medical school, ostensibly because the cumbersome name "Mahsereghian" might prove too difficult for his patients to say or spell.

In hindsight, I wondered if there might not have been more to that story. What role might the fear of prejudice have played in my father's decision to change his name, that and the natural inclination to want to fit in with the white Anglo-Saxon medical culture in which he found himself? Would patients in our predominantly white, middle-class town have wanted the doctor with the strange last name delivering their babies in the 1940s and 1950s?

Like my parents, it was easy for me to hide behind my Anglicized last name. When people asked, as they always did, about the origin of my unusual first name, I easily explained it away with the glib response, "Oh, it's a family name." Besides, I lacked most Armenians' signature bulbous nose and pale white skin and was more often taken for Mexican, the more prevalent ethnic group in our town.

Now I was at Mijares with Grandmother Jemela speaking to me again, this time through Raven, and asking me to write a book.

Heal her and write a book? I thought incredulously. What on earth does that mean?

I was forced to recognize that maybe there was a reason I'd lugged myself over to Mijares that Friday night after all.

Chapter 3

Early Days

I was a chubby child with cherubic brown curls, often alone in the sanctuary of my sky-blue bedroom. I would lie on my bed for hours and gaze out the bedroom window that stretched across one wall. Outside, a twisted bamboo forest hid flowers of many types pushing up through the grass beneath its stalks. Every April, white calla lilies sprung up beside the stone walkway just beyond the bamboo, and I would count them. They seemed like friends. When not lost in thought, gazing at the forest, I lay on my twin bed with the quilted blue coverlet, writing in my journal or reading endless books of fiction, transporting myself into worlds not my own.

My other friend was food. Stolen food, sneaked into my bedroom when my very busy mother wasn't looking. Empty bowls of Carnation chocolate ice cream hidden under the bed, pieces of Oscar Mayer bologna rolled up with bright yellow Gulden's mustard oozing out the ends, Oreos stolen from my mother's carefully constructed hiding place, and anything else I could sneak from the kitchen down the long hall into my little blue bedroom. These escapades were surreptitious and often nocturnal. They were frantic searches for love in a bottle, wrapper, or ice cream carton, devoured before anyone might walk down the hall, barge into my room, and find the wrappings of my crimes.

Shame and need all wrapped up together.

I was a sensitive little girl who craved the company and attention of just about anyone. But there never seemed to be anyone around. Where was everyone?

Outside the walls of my room, Mom scurried about cleaning, shopping, cooking, and perfecting the world around her. She often seemed tense and anxious. Anything could set her off: a dish left on the counter, a hair out of place, an outfit not perfectly matched. Anything. I feared her anger and learned to be very quiet and to stay out of everyone's way, especially hers.

My sister Lynne, nine years older than me, was either at school or out with friends, out with a boyfriend, or sometimes just out getting into trouble. On a few occasions, when my father came home from work, I remember him punishing her for being bad, for crashing his car when she was only fifteen before she had her driver's license, or going out on a date with her English teacher. It was louder when Lynne was around. She and Mom seemed to butt heads at every turn. Their frequent fighting unnerved me, and often sent me fleeing back to my little blue bedroom.

I also had two older brothers. The most senior, Bud, spent a lot of time building things in the lower garage at the bottom of the property: waterskis and items made of wood. Sometimes he would stay there all day and forget to eat, and I would go down to see if he needed something. I didn't really understand anyone who could forget to eat.

My other brother, Jim, closest to me in age, lived for sports. He had a transistor radio glued to his ear, listening to the California Angels in baseball season, the Lakers in basketball season, and the USC Trojans during football season. I had a crush on all his cute, athletic friends, but they mostly never gave me the time of day. I wasn't like all the leggy, blonde cheerleader types with whom he and his friends hung out.

Dad worked as an obstetrician-gynecologist in the nearby town of Pasadena. It seemed as if everything transpired to prepare the house, the kids, and the world for when Dad returned home from work around 6:30 each evening. Mom prepared a gourmet Armenian meal; I set the table as perfectly as I could and placed the bourbon, water, ice, and glass on the kitchen counter for his nightly cocktails. Mom rid Dad's study of all dogs and children and placed the carefully folded evening newspaper next to his armchair. Mom's world, our world, *the* whole world seemed to revolve around Dad. Everyone, including me, loved and revered him.

———————————

Growing up in Altadena in the 1960s, it seemed exotic to be Armenian. In those days, few people had heard of us, so it seemed cool. Indeed, the few people who knew that we were Armenian didn't seem to mind, and I had a friend or two in the neighborhood who were also Armenian. We only spoke English, however. My parents sometimes lapsed into Turkish or Armenian when they didn't want us to understand something. Bud's best friend Dick taught me how to swear in Armenian, but other than that, it was all English.

Mom once said that when she started grammar school in Albany, New York, she only spoke Armenian and not English, so I figured that's what they had spoken in her house growing up. But no one ever actually taught us any Turkish or Armenian. Those were my parent's secret languages.

Three of my four grandparents came from a town called Aintab in Turkey, but no one ever spoke much about Aintab or the old country or how or why they came to New York. Indeed, no one I knew had ever been to Aintab or anywhere in Turkey, and as far as I knew, no one wanted to go.

It would be many years before I heard anything about the starving Armenians and the massive genocide that killed 1.5 million of us between 1895 and 1920. Those lucky enough to survive the long death marches into the desert or to escape past Turkey's borders by some other means formed the Armenian diaspora in Syria, Iran, Lebanon, New York, Europe, and South America. That diaspora would figure prominently in my later personal and professional life. But, in those early days, I knew little about the genocide or how it silently impacted our everyday life.

Chapter 4

Sunday Afternoons

I sit, mostly naked and cross-legged, in the moist, dark earth under one of the four orange trees lining our backyard. I'm dressed in nothing but a cloth diaper. Dew drips from the branches overhead on this clear, bright December morning. Johno reaches into the branches and picks an orange with his hand. Dead leaves crunch under his feet as he walks toward me, peeling the orange with his pocket knife, one vertical section after another. He pulls the orange into halves, spilling juice all over us, separates a small section, and hands it to me. He sits beside me, and our "orange party" begins. He smiles down at me, his deep brown eyes laughing, and calls me "Chuchilik," his Armenian term of endearment for me. I don't know what it means. I only know that I feel loved and special whenever he says it. I look up at him adoringly. The tree branches bend low, heavy with fruit, and the smell of orange blossoms permeates the air. I feel happy and loved. It is the fondest memory of my childhood.

Johno was twenty-two years old, tall with wavy brown hair and strong, broad shoulders. He had arrived the year before from Aleppo, Syria, to live with us, sponsored by my parents. His father, Artin, was Grandmother Jemela's brother. Uncle Artin had fled Aintab four decades earlier and gone into the Syrian desert with his four siblings before the worst of the genocide broke out. Family lore has it that a friendly Turk, aware of the massacres and exportations to come, had warned my great-grandfather to flee with his family.

Johno was the first of my father's cousins to emigrate to the U.S. After Johno came his brother Albert from Paris and then Berj from Beirut. The last to arrive was his sister Laurance with her four daughters from Aleppo. With their thick accents, black hair, white skin, and boisterous laughter, this extended family became my old country cousins. Most of the rest of my family, except older aunts and uncles, had been born in the U.S. Johno and his family felt like real Armenians to me, unlike the tan, California-speaking, bleached blonde, mini-skirt-wearing members of the rest of my family.

On many Sunday afternoons during my early years, Johno and his siblings would gather at our place for dinner with the rest of the family, including my Aunty Gladys and Uncle Henry with my cousin Carol, my widowed great aunts Bea and Flo, and Aunty Vic and Uncle Mike and their kids.

Mom would begin preparing the Sunday feast mid-week, sitting at the kitchen table rolling beef, spices, and white rice into pickled grape leaves three inches long. She'd stack the grape leaves, called "sarma," four or five high in a large, round copper-bottomed pan and cover it with a white plate. I sometimes sat at the table watching her roll the sarma into the tight green cylinders, but I was never allowed to help. My rolling strategies never seemed to measure up to Mom's impeccable standards.

On Saturday afternoons, Mom and I drove south a mile to the Little Armenia of Pasadena to stock up for the Sunday afternoon dinner. This was before the massive influx of Persian, Lebanese, and Russian Armenians into the nearby cities of Glendale and Hollywood.

On that three-block stretch stood the Sevan Bakery, Pano's Lahmejoun shop, Garo's Basturma shop, and Good Foods—our local Armenian food stores. Good Foods sat on the corner of Washington and Allen streets, as it still does, and was the only full-service Armenian grocery store in town. We'd walk in, Mom in her two-inch Adrienne Eiger black pumps, plaid wool blazer, and tailored Evan Picone pants. Like a bull charging her prey, she walked quickly, head down, and tilted forward. Her blonde hair, coiffed in a short bob, stood out among the dark hair and eyes of the cashiers and the butcher offering up his lamb shanks and beefsteaks. I trailed hesitantly, in my oversized, fraying Champion sweatshirt and shapeless bell-bottom corduroys, eying the exotic wares out of the corner of my eye and trying desperately not to be seen.

To the left of the entrance stood a nook devoted entirely to sleek, silver Turkish coffee pots, tiny porcelain espresso cups painted with delicate pink and green flowers, and their accompanying 5-inch round saucers, all unfamiliar to me. I particularly loved looking at the porcelain cups, one-quarter the size of the coffee cups we had at home, almost small enough to fit in a doll's house.

The aisles crowded together, goods of every kind stacked dense and high on the peeling shelves and any available floor space. Cellophane packets of hot Aleppo peppers and dried mint hung from little silver hooks next to freshly baked loaves of lavash in two-inch-high rectangles and baklava in every shape and size. Tins of olives and bottles of olive oil from Greece and Turkey lined one aisle, and cookies and candy tins emblazoned with an exotic script I couldn't decipher on others. Twenty-pound burlap bags of flour, garbanzo beans, rice in small, medium, and large grains, and bulgur lay on the ground, crowding the slender aisles even more. The smell of what we then called Turkish coffee and the exotic spices of sumac and cardamom permeated the air. It felt like a foreign country, fascinating yet strange. I watched as the employees' black eyes examined us suspiciously. We looked like strangers in their land, too.

Mom strode up to the glassed-in butcher counter with quick, staccato Armenian words I could not understand shooting off her tongue. She pointed her index finger at a particular slab of basturma. I watched as all eyes in the store jerked toward her, this fashionably dressed blonde ordering in brisk Armenian. I didn't know whether to be proud or embarrassed.

Then she'd turn quickly to me, effortlessly code-switching into curt, clipped English: "Jemela, go over and get me a few packages of lavash and some fresh string cheese. Don't get the already wrapped cheese in the plastic, but the fresh pieces in brown paper. And be sure the bread is fresh. Touch it to make sure it bounces back. Hurry."

Like a docile doe, I hurried toward the string cheese counter.

My job on Sundays was to prepare the hors-d'oeuvres tray, separating the cheese, the pita bread, my Dad's homemade olives, the pickled vegetables, and the basturma into separate little compartments on the round green revolving tray. The old aunties would pinch my cheeks and say "Yavriges," sweetheart, to me in Armenian as I handed them each a cocktail napkin and proudly held the tray for them to sample. Mom and the other women would race around the kitchen, putting rice pilaf on to boil, drizzling a syrup of honey and water on the home-made baklava, tending the sarma pot on the stove, and readying the long skewers of shish kebab, onions, and tomatoes for the barbecue out back in the patio.

Earlier in the day, Mom and I would have set the long table in the dining room with the lace tablecloth her mother had brought from the old country with the good china and good silver my parents had received as wedding gifts. Every piece had to be correctly placed—the water and wine glasses above the knife, the salad plate above the fork, the napkins set with the crease facing the salad fork, and the steak knife blade facing inward to the right of the silver-rimmed beige china. Fresh roses in every color, picked from our garden, flowed from a crystal vase in the center of the table. Earlier in the day, I would carefully rake the thick white shag carpet in the white-domed living room and scrub all the bathroom mirrors with Windex.

As the women tended to the food, the men gathered around the barbecue on the flagstone patio, drinking bourbon and gin, smoking cigars, laughing and telling jokes, and waiting for the raw shish kebab to arrive from the kitchen.

I loved to infiltrate the group of men and listen to their conversations. Those conversations always seemed more interesting to me than the frenetic talk of recipes and cooking of the women. I would carry my hors-d'oeuvres tray down the steep steps to the patio and ceremoniously offer it to the men: Dad, Uncle Henry, Johno, Albert, Berj, and my dad's cousin Hank. Johno would look over at me and say with a twinkle in his eye, "Be careful, Chuchilik, or we're gonna barbecue you." That terrified me. For years, I had nightmares of the wolf from Little Red Riding Hood chasing me around the barbecue, trying to catch me to roast me over the hot coals. I always considered these barbecue dreams precursors to my lifelong dislike of beef and lamb. That and Dad's tendency to char the meat, which pretty much tasted burnt to me.

With the meat cooked and each salad plate carefully filled, we placed the steaming plates of kebab, sarma, and pilaf in the center of the table where everyone could reach them.

After everyone was seated, we'd fold our hands in front of us and say Grace: "Bless, oh Lord, this food to our use and our hearts to thy service. We ask this in Christ's name. Amen." I stifled my nightly desire to giggle or rush through the prayer lest I endure my father's withering glance. I always tried to nab the seat right next to Dad. His solid presence calmed the hectic anxiety that had descended during the women's mad race to get everything cooked, plated, and onto the table at one time.

After the baklava and coffee had been served, the men retired to my father's study at the far end of the house for more cigars and TV. Portly Uncle Henry could always be found dozing on the couch with his pants undone, his ample belly spilling out over his loosened belt.

The women, at least the younger of us, hastily cleared all the plates and glasses from the table. We carefully rinsed and washed every plate, piece of silverware, and glass by hand in hot soapy water and passed them to the next person to dry. The same with the pots and pans. After all the dishes were put away, we sponged down the kitchen, leaving the stoves and countertops gleaming. It was a laborious ritual that I relished, enjoying the company of my older cousins and aunts and making me feel industrious and important.

I loved these Sunday dinners; the soft murmur of Turkish and Armenian spoken in the background, the old aunties pinching my cheeks and telling me how cute I was, the heaping plates of food, and the sweet smell of cigar smoke.

But afterward, after the extended family had kissed and hugged everyone goodbye and taken their leave, the familiar loneliness would set in, and I would find myself back in my little blue room alone. Mom and Dad collapsed from fatigue in the study, and my siblings dispersed to I know not where. I just knew that life was back to normal, and I didn't much like it.

Chapter 5

On Deafness

*Every one of us is blind and deaf until our eyes are opened to our fellow-
men, until our ears hear the voice of humanity.*
~Helen Keller

I tossed and turned, alone in the matchbox-sized cubicle masquerad-
ing as a hotel room on the outskirts of New Delhi. Sleep evaded me.
The lumps in the narrow bed bore into muscles bruised from bumping
along dirt roads in ancient rickshaws on the streets of old Delhi. My
white Lucite alarm clock, a traveling companion since my first year of
college, sat beside me on the rickety bedside table. The little clock
drilled her shrill cadence into my brain, awakening me from my fitful
sleep. I turned over to try to escape her blows when suddenly, there
was silence. What had happened to the ticking? I started experiment-
ing, laying my head on one side of the bed and then the other, covering
one ear at a time to see if I could hear her. I could hear nothing when
laying on my left ear; on my right, her clamoring assaulted my soul.

Wow, I thought, I can't hear anything from my right ear.

I was 27 and alone in my tiny matchbox. In the 2 a.m. darkness, I
chuckled to myself. How had this happened? When had it happened?
Had I listened too loudly to Joni Mitchell and Jackson Browne, singing
along with them at the top of my lungs for too many years? Or had I
been deaf since birth and not known? I couldn't recall ever having been
to an ear doctor or having a hearing test. As the daughter of a physician, I rarely visited them, relying on Dad for all my medical needs.

Dad had been deaf in his right ear since birth, or at least since I was born. We had befriended his deaf ear and honored it as a part of our family.

Maybe I inherited Dad's bad ear. That would be fine with me. Anything that made me remotely like Dad was okay with me. With his soft, sparkling eyes and quiet ways, Dad had always been my role model. We both loved to read and grapple with big ideas and could often be brought to tears by a touching TV commercial or a sentimental gesture from a friend.

At the time, this discovery was more humorous to me than disturbing. Having grown up with a half-deaf dad, I knew that I could survive perfectly well with only one functioning ear. I quickly adapted to any situation, seating myself to the right of friends at dinner or cocking my left ear toward my clients while working.

I had never thought about what deafness might mean for us. What might our deaf ears be trying to tell us? What had I not heard in my life? What had I not wanted to hear? What might my father not have heard? Indeed, I had never heard stories of my ancestors or the genocide that killed so many of them. No stories told, no stories heard.

In my therapy office, I keep a small white porcelain statue of Kuan Yin hidden at the back of a compartment in my desk. A larger wooden version sits atop the piano in my living room, keeping watch over us. Another, fashioned of grey sandstone, perches in our front yard, welcoming visitors and reminding us of the need for compassion.

Kuan Yin is the female Bodhisattva who hears the cries of the world. I have devoted my life to hearing the world's cries, or so I have thought. My physician father dedicated his life to hearing other cries, the cries of newborn babies taking their first breath. I wonder what cries we failed to hear. Indeed, Dad often could not hear my cries when I went to him or Mom with them.

I arrived in India after six weeks in neighboring Pakistan on a Fulbright grant for teachers of culture to study Islam. At the time, I was teaching English as a Second Language and Cross-Culture Communication at the University of Southern California in exchange for my Ph.D. courses in Counseling Psychology.

I had never intended to study Islam or visit Pakistan. I had applied to study Buddhism in India, sent, I thought, by Kuan Yin to hear the cries of the poor and the wisdom of the spiritually awakened. I was taken aback when the man from the Fulbright Commission in Washington, DC, called to ask if I would consider going to Pakistan instead.

"Well, I'd rather go to India," I'd responded.

"The Indian trip is full, so we're offering you a grant to study in Pakistan," he replied. Fate and Kuan Yin apparently had other ideas. Never one to turn down an all-expenses paid trip to a far-off land, I said, "Sure. I'll go to Pakistan."

I had arranged to meet one of my Indian students, Surendra, in New Delhi after the six-week study tour through Pakistan. That's when I discovered my deaf ear.

What else had drawn me to the Indian subcontinent? I had always been interested in the world's religions, and it was trendy in the 1970s and 1980s to meditate and study Eastern philosophy and everything Indian. But I was looking for something more, something primal, something far removed from the sanitized, sparkling, beautiful world of Southern California. I just didn't know it at the time.

I had never felt at home in Southern California, if not the proverbial fish out of water, then a monkey trapped in the zoo craving the freedom of the jungle. I didn't know why my father's family relocated from New York City to Pasadena, California. The likely story was its proximity to relatives already living in the area. But once here, my mother, in particular, sought to fit in as much as she could, dying her naturally dark hair blonde and cropping her sizable Armenian nose into a pert little upswing.

I saw her wedding pictures for the first time as an adult, shocked at a version of myself staring back at me: deep brown eyes and long, wavy dark hair with a prominent, if not bulbous, nose. The mother I had always known had short blonde hair, coiffed by Nina at the Hair Palace every Friday. Mom liked to brag that she weighed 107 pounds on the day she married, extremely lean on her 5'8" frame. Dad had pinned a picture of her in a bathing suit on the inside of his locker at the County Hospital where he worked, a Rita Hayworth lookalike that both embarrassed and thrilled Mom. Mom took great pride in her svelte figure, loved clothes, and was the best-dressed and most outgoing woman in every room. She valiantly tried to pass down her values about appearances and charm to her four children.

To me, it seemed as if Mom sometimes turned her new American nose up at some of the other Armenians in our town, complaining about their requests for money or how they dressed and failed to do their hair. She seemed disdainful of the few Armenians living near us and chose to associate with my father's medical colleagues instead. Later, I understood Mom's derision of her people as a possible defense against shame, her shame at coming from an immigrant family, being Other, and having grown up poor in her early years. Her shame seemed to strike at the very core of her being, although I doubt she was ever aware of it.

Looking back, I think Mom's discomfort with herself, and mine, of the glitzy, materialistic world of Southern California pushed me out into the wider world, searching for something Mom strived hard to leave behind. Thus I went looking in Pakistan and India, as I had earlier in Spain and Italy and as I would later in China and South America.

As a young woman in college in the late 1970s, I chaired and helped found the feminist organization on our small liberal arts campus in Colorado. I eschewed the world of beer pong, sororities, and frat parties. I preferred talking deep into the night about the ideas of French philosopher Simone De Beauvoir and American feminist poet Adrienne Rich. When I returned to Southern California in my 20s to pursue graduate studies, I lived alone in an upstairs studio apartment for many years.

Independent young woman that I had become, I feared my reaction to the culture of Pakistan, a conservative Islamic country. In 1983, observant Pakistani women donned full-length burqas to shield themselves from the gazes of passing men. A mesh screen sown into the burqa at eye level provided their singular vision of the outside world. They were only allowed to speak to men outside of their family if a male family member was present, and they seldom left the house alone.

To my mind, they lived shackled and oppressed. While walking through the streets of Pakistan with my male colleagues, I fended off male stares as I bounced along in my knee-length, cotton, sleeveless dresses, talking animatedly to whatever man I accompanied. When I asked our leader about the looks, he responded that, most likely, the

staring men considered me a whore for being out in the street uncovered and speaking loudly to a man. This statement affirmed every neg-
ative stereotype I had of Pakistan.

But the gentleness and hospitality of the people humbled me. Rather than Osama bin Laden's terrorists or the fierce, fighting tribes of
the northern regions I had read so much about, I found kindness. This
kindness surprised me. While talking with a young woman about my
age, her long, dark locks covered by a silky shawl, she smiled sweetly
and, with a twinkle in her eye, said, "My children are my Ph.D." It took
a while for this comment to sink in. When it did, I felt embarrassed
and ashamed of my assumptions about her life.

The few academic women we met talked sadly about their inability
to find husbands willing to marry successful, highly educated women.
I recalled my mother warning me of the same possibility when I told
her I wanted to pursue a Ph.D. "Jemela," she had scowled, "you're
educating yourself out of the marriage market. No man is ever going
to want to marry you now." Mom's comment stunned and angered me.
Now, in Pakistan, I felt compassion for these educated women unable
to find husbands. Yet I could also feel their pride in educating themselves against all odds. The conflicting emotions whirled inside me,
confusing me and bumping up against the simple worldview I had constructed for myself before arriving. I realized that I was not so different
from these women after all.

While there, at five designated times throughout the day, the lilting
Muslim call to prayer rang out from the minarets atop every
mosque. As the first tones began, the observant stopped their daily
activities, placed a small prayer rug on the ground facing Mecca, knelt
upon it, and rested their heads on the ground to recite holy verses from
the Koran. Though I failed to understand the lilting Arabic cadence,
the mournful dirge struck something deep within me, some long-
dormant longing. For what? Connection to something greater than
myself? Some genetic remnant passed on from my grandparents' days
in Islamic Turkey? I wasn't sure. I just knew I loved it. I had wanted
to go to India to find a spiritual connection but heard it in Pakistan
instead, amidst the Muslim minarets and the call to prayer.

After arriving in India, certain images seared themselves into my memory.

Withered old women with leathered visages lifting saris faded by the incessant sun, squatting in the middle of the road, leaving their excrement and urine to run down the gutters. Brides seated alone in gilded cages resting on the shoulders of male family members riding nervously to the homes of their prospective bridegrooms, the curtains of their chariots blowing against their bejeweled faces. Gongs and bells of well-wishers clamored beside them, scenting the air with the petals of pink, white, and red roses strewn along the pathway.

Cows and pigs roamed the streets alongside modern high rises, leaving their mud pies to rot and stink in the streets, creating the pervasive smell of urine and feces. Rickshaws on the backs of perpetually bent older men ferried passengers along roads crowded with cars, animals, and streaming bodies. Ringing rickshaw bells and blaring car horns provided the soundtrack for the harried scene. Beggars appeared at every turn, asking for a rupee or a bit of naan.

The streets of Old Delhi assaulted my senses, leaving me paralyzed. One day, my limbs and body literally froze with pain, refusing to move. I couldn't walk or eat—all I could do was lay prostrate in my bed. My breathing became labored, and I didn't leave my room for three days. I became fearful of what was happening to me. Was I going crazy? I had heard many tourists were sickened while in India, but I hadn't expected this. I could only conclude that India herself had overwhelmed me, stopping me in my tracks.

But what did She want from me, this vast, pulsating country? What was she trying to say by visiting this sickness upon me? Had I heard and seen too much to tolerate, or was she asking me to pause, to pay attention, and to listen more closely to her life surging around me?

I had no idea.

I wonder now, though, if my family's silence, their deafness to our history, might have stemmed from a similar pain, a pain too great for the body and soul to assimilate.

———

More than anything, I wanted to go to the holy town of Varanasi in Northern India on the banks of the sacred Ganges River. Buddha is thought to have preached his first sermon in Varanasi, birthing what would later become Buddhism.

On our first day there, my traveling partner Surendra and I awakened at 5 a.m. to taxi to the banks of the river. A grey tin boat with a white outboard motor carried us onto the gentle dawn ripples. Steps lined the wall at the water's edge, moving some twenty feet into the water. Half-naked men in dirty off-white dhotis waded down the steps and dunked their heads three times into the murky river. Indian lore holds that to bathe in the Ganges cleanses one of the sins accrued over many lifetimes, wiping clean the karmic slate. Women dressed in full saris did the same, sometimes wading until the water covered their shoulders before dunking their heads into the early dawn. I watched transfixed, wanting yet not wanting to join them in the water to cleanse myself of my own transgressions.

Along the banks of the river, tall funeral pyres known as burning ghats rested on stacks of dark brown logs, waiting for the processions of the dead to reach them. Indian men carried bodies wrapped in white muslin on wooden pallets through the streets of Varanasi, held aloft on their way to the ghats like the brides traveling to meet their grooms. After arriving, the bodies were stretched atop the pyres and lit, the plumes of fire licking the rising sun as the bodies slowly burned. The acrid smell of smoke and burning flesh permeated the air that blackened the rising sun.

I stared silently as the bodies atop the ghats slowly turned to ash. As I sat in our little boat, a naked, bloated male body floated down the river before us. He looked to be in his 30s, his bulbous head completely bald and his limbs bruised blue and black. My stomach lurched. I asked the driver of our skiff why this man had not been burned and instead drifted naked down the river. He said that criminals and prisoners were not given the honor of burning on the funeral pyres and were thrown into the river instead.

That image of the bald head and bruised arms not allowed their proper cremation, drifting through the brown, murky water at dawn, has stayed with me for over 35 years.

As a child, I feared death above all. Do all children fear death, or was I unique in my palpable, conscious fear of it? I didn't fear my death as much as that of my loved ones, particularly my father. How would I, could I, survive his death? I often wondered. Watching the dead carried through the streets of India, and staring transfixed as their limbs slowly enflamed, brought me face to face with this fear in a strangely comforting way. I had craved this meeting, this confrontation, and this knowledge of death up close. I didn't know why at the time, but now I wonder if it wasn't a yearning to hear, to see, and to experience that which could never be spoken of in my family, that which had happened long before in another far-off land.

In India, as in Pakistan, I felt a part of something primal and close to the earth, intimately connected to life's daily thrums and rituals. I heard life in all its blaring cacophony. I saw death as an everyday oc-currence, confronting it head-on in ways I never had and would never experience in Southern California. I didn't so much hear the world's cries as hear and experience the sacredness of life in all its ordinariness. I also heard how much more alike we humans are than different, no matter our external circumstances. For that, I am profoundly grateful. Grateful to Kuan Yin and the Fulbright Commission, and whatever other fates may have intervened in sending me to both Pakistan and India in that summer of 1983.

Chapter 6

Glendale

G lendale was the last place I wanted to work after my years-long slog toward psychology licensure. In 1992, my friend Reese, a fellow psychologist, called one day and asked if I wanted to look at an available office in her suite in downtown Glendale, CA. I had just completed the arduous exams required to become a California psychologist. I was eager to move on from the counseling center where I had been a psychological assistant for six years.

"Well, I'm really not interested in working in Glendale," I told her.

I had grown up in the multiracial, diverse community of Altadena and had no interest in opening my first independent office in a suburb known historically for its white, conservative, "John Bircher" views. Not too many years before, it had been considered dangerous for people of color to even walk through the streets of Glendale at night.

"C'mon Jemela, just take a look," Reese pleaded. "It's a really nice office. I think you might like it."

So I made the fifteen-minute drive south to see Reese's office. A mirrored, polished mahogany-paneled elevator whisked me to the second floor of the brick facade building. The office stood directly across from the elevator. A brass plaque on the wall next to the dark wood double doors read "Psychological Associates." As I entered the waiting room, cool teal walls, the smell of fresh paint, and huge picture windows overlooking wispy green branches met my critical gaze. Classical music wafted throughout the suite, decorated with abstracts by Klee and Chagall. I'd seen that cafés, restaurants, and movie houses lined the recently refurbished cobblestoned street in front of the office, and colorful flowers decorated the block's median. Willow trees swayed curbside in the spring breeze, brushing against the second-story windows. This clearly wasn't the Glendale of my 1960s youth.

What's more, since the late 1970s, Glendale had become home to more than 80,000 Armenians, the largest concentration of Armenians in the world outside of the country of Armenia itself. The first set of more recent Armenians came to Glendale after Ayatollah Khomeini's Islamic Revolution in Iran ousted the Western-oriented Shah. Stripped of all their possessions and in danger once again because of their Christian faith, those who could afford to fled Iran.

In the 1980s, a new flood of refugees came, escaping the civil war in Lebanon and another from Russia with the fall of the Soviet Empire in the 1990s. I had been aware of the influx of immigrant Armenians moving into Glendale eight years before when I had done my clinical internship at a local Glendale hospital.

At least on a conscious level, the Armenian diaspora outside my office door had nothing to do with my decision to say yes to Reese and open shop in downtown Glendale. No, the big picture window, light-drenched waiting room, and lively cafés lining the street below had seduced me. Or so I thought.

Across the street from my new office, black-eyed men smoking cigars and women with cascading dark locks in tight jeans and tall stilettos sat outside a coffeehouse drinking steaming cups of espresso and nibbling on baklava. URARTU was spelled in tall black letters over the brick facade of the coffeehouse. In free moments between clients, I peered down at the gesticulating hands and lively conversations of the patrons clustered at the small outside tables and wondered about their lives. I had no idea what "Urartu" meant, but it was clear from the clientele parading in and out of its doors that this café was an Armenian gathering place.

I later learned that Urartu was an ancient, lost civilization between 860 BC and 550 BC near the site of Mt. Ararat in Western Armenia. It was reputed to be the birthplace of present-day Armenia. The irony of my ending up across from this particular cafe in Glendale was lost on me at the time. Only now do I wonder if fate brought me into the heart of this immigrant Armenian community. During the nineteen years I worked out of this office in downtown Glendale, I learned more about my culture, history, and heritage than I had learned in my first 37 years.

Eight years before, while working as an intern at the Family Practice Residency Program of Glendale Adventist Hospital, I had become aware of the rift between the wealthy, white population of old Glendale and the new Armenian immigrants. Unaware of my Armenian heritage, older white clients would complain incessantly about the new foreigners taking over their city, foreigners who refused to learn English, pushed their way to the front of every grocery store line, yelled angrily, and liberally used government Medicaid benefits while dripping in handmade gold jewelry from the old country.

I remember the biker dude who rode up to the clinic one day on his Harley, his long, straggly beard flowing. He flopped down on the sofa in my office, saying, "I'm here to talk about the AAA."

"The Automobile Club of America?" I asked quizzically.

"No, the Armenian Assholes of America."

I was taken aback but, in my best intern-trying-to-act-professional voice, responded, "Oh, I see. Would you like to tell me more about that?"

The staff of the Residency Program where I worked, made up mainly of Caucasian medical residents and attending physicians, seemed even angrier.

"They're pushy, they talk too loud, take too much time, and are never satisfied."

One resident physician, exasperated by dealing with this alien population, once said to me, "Jemela, if you had an "ian" (the common suffice in most Armenian names indicating their origin) at the end of your name, no one would ever talk to you." So I took my identity underground, never telling my clients or even some of my colleagues my ethnic background or the origins of my grandparents.

My collision with the Armenian world of Glendale created a swirling maelstrom of conflicting emotions within me. Mainly I was confused. I understood the objections of my medical colleagues and tried to empathize with them as they sought to work with this strange new population. On a deeper level, though, I felt shame and embarrassment. Embarrassment for my identification with this loathed group and humiliation that my ethnic group was so maligned. I didn't know with whom to align myself: the medical staff I belonged to or the patients with whom I shared a culture and heritage. I bounced from one side of the mandorla to the other, never finding that sweet spot of integration within its center.

My confusion became so great that I returned to that family medicine center a couple of years later to write my doctoral dissertation on the interaction between Armenian patients and their American healthcare professionals: I titled it, *Frustration and Prejudice Development in a Family Health Clinic: An Ethnographic Analysis of the Effects of an Influx of Immigrant Armenians upon Healthcare Relationships.*

In so many ways, I was desperate to understand who I was.

Years later, I asked myself, what if I'd never accepted that psychology internship at the Glendale Adventist Medical Center when I was finishing my doctoral studies?

I had never heard of the Glendale Adventist Medical Center. Heck, I wasn't even looking for an internship. One of my professors came to me and suggested I apply. I had no idea why she asked me instead of the dozens of her other graduate students. I didn't learn until years later that her partner ran the behavioral health department there, giving her a significant connection to it.

I had no idea that in accepting that internship, I'd be walking into the largest community of immigrant Armenians in the world outside of Armenia.

Did the behavioral health team know I was Armenian-American before interviewing me? Did they even know they had a problem with the Armenian patients then? Did they know I knew little about being Armenian or didn't speak the language? Again, I have no idea.

During that year, I met some of the multitudes of immigrant Armenian patients who had recently moved to Glendale from all parts of the war-torn, troubled world. There, for the first time, I felt myself occupying two worlds simultaneously, the world of the American health care professional and the world of the ethnically Armenian. There, these two worlds collided.

For the first time, I also became aware of the immense pride these Armenian people, who felt Other to me, took in their heritage and identities as Armenians. While I lived in a primarily American world, they seemed to live in a predominantly Armenian world by choice, socializing only with other Armenians, attending Armenian churches and schools, and speaking the language almost exclusively.

At the Glendale Adventist Medical Center, I met the Armenian Other outside of myself and, as a consequence, began to engage this Other within myself. This clash proved instrumental in starting me on the path toward the integration of these two worlds within me.

I also learned that it's wise to listen to the clues, the innuendos, and the invitations that the Universe places in our paths. Follow her breadcrumbs, I learned, for they may lead us to places in our lives we never knew we needed to go.

Chapter 7

Taline

Soon after I moved into my new office, a friend called and asked if I would be willing to work with the cousin of one of her friends. "She needs someone to talk to," the friend murmured. "I think you'd be a good fit."

The following Wednesday morning at 10:10, I opened my office door to an olive-skinned, willowy young woman sitting rigidly upright in one of our teal and pink wing chairs, twisting her hands nervously in her lap. Her heavily eyelined chestnut eyes flitted between the Miros and Chagalls on the waiting room walls. A mane of gently wavy black hair brushed her face and fell below her collarbones. Her perfectly creased cream silk blouse lay tucked neatly into her skintight Joe's jeans, hugging her ankles above strappy, high-heeled black sandals. As she walked into the office, I caught a whiff of musky Opium perfume overlaying the dank smell of cigarettes and recently consumed espresso, probably from Urartu across the street. Once in the office, she glanced suspiciously around as if looking for something and haltingly asked, "Can anyone hear us in here?"

She fingered a pair of black onyx worry beads, moving the tiny beads back and forth across a silver chain as she began, often in a whisper, to tell me her story.

Taline had just turned 28. She lived with her family of four in the south of Glendale and had emigrated from Damascus when she was two. She was engaged to a 32-year-old Armenian accountant named

Berge, a boy she had met in the Armenian grammar school they had both attended. They were slated to marry the following year. After graduating from USC with a graphic design degree, Taline worked in marketing for a local Armenian business owned by one of her father's friends.

Though Taline spoke English perfectly, having grown up in Glendale, I would listen attentively to the lilting tones of Armenian which emanated from her on those rare occasions when she answered her phone in session. I understood that she spoke Armenian with her friends and family but always English with me as I didn't speak Armenian. The life Taline's immigrant parents had hoped for and dreamed for her had come true: an education at the prestigious local university, a good job, and now an engagement to a stable, hardworking Armenian young man.

But Taline had secretly fallen in love with Erica, a young odar (non-Armenian) filmmaker she had met in a UCLA Extension course. With her colorful tattoos, gold nose ring, unruly blonde curls, and hipster bohemian dresses, Erica was everything Berge was not. Berge spoke in kind cadences, was quiet and studious, and wore large, square-rimmed black glasses. He favored khaki pants and neatly ironed button-down blue shirts. He dutifully took Taline to a local Armenian restaurant for dinner every Wednesday night. They spent weekends with one or the other of their families, drinking arak, a pungent Armenian brandy, and playing backgammon. Each night after saying goodnight to their parents, Berge would begin to kiss her gently, leading to a "make out" session that Taline never allowed to get past what we used to call "second base" in elementary school. Taline had been a virgin when she met Erica, but that had changed six months before our meeting. She and Erica would steal away to art galleries and independent film houses during long lunch hours. On those evenings, when she told her parents she needed to work late for a deadline, they spent hours talking about music, literature, and philosophy.

Erica shared a loft in downtown LA with several artist friends and did freelance film work when she could get it. At Erica's loft, Taline discovered a passion she hadn't begun to experience with Berge. Erica longed to meet Taline's parents and become a more significant part of her life, coaxing her to leave Berge and deepen their love. Recently, Taline had developed insomnia and began to eat excessively and then purge to maintain her slender figure. Her internal dilemma had begun to play itself out in her body.

Taline had sought counseling to talk about this challenging situation. She had shared her relationship with Erica with no one save one of her best female friends and definitely needed someone to talk with. She loved Berge, who felt like family, but she was passionately in love with Erica. Should she continue to lie to her family and keep seeing Erica or break it off with Erica and marry Berge? The dilemma riddled her with guilt and uncertainty.

Taline's grandparents and extended family hailed from Diyarbakir in Eastern Turkey. Her family spoke of this area not as Turkey but as Western Armenia, referring to its historical roots as Armenian lands before the Turks claimed the area for their own. Like many other Armenians at that time, her grandparents fled to Syria after the 1915 Armenian Genocide. She once told me that the Turks had murdered dozens of her male Armenian relatives during the genocide.

Taline's extended family belonged to an Armenian political group that sought revenge against the Turks who had massacred their people, setting up covert operations and quietly assassinating Turkish diplomats throughout the world. Taline's brother Alex had fought in the 1992 war in Nagorno-Karabakh to claim Armenian lands back from Azerbaijan and continued to be active politically in Armenian politics.

Her family often traveled to Armenia to visit friends and family. Taline had grown up surrounded by fellow Armenians in Glendale and socialized almost exclusively with Armenians. When she spoke about the genocide, it was as if it had happened to her, not some long-lost relatives she had never met. It lived in her body and her soul. How could she betray her family and culture by leaving Berge to be with Erica?

Taline lived in an entirely Armenian world, though it lay tucked away in a corner of Southern California. Her relationship with Erica threatened to shatter this protected existence. Would she be able to bring a non-Armenian woman into her world? Would Erica fit in? Would her parents disown her? These were the questions with which she grappled.

Taline's world seemed alien, yet fascinating to me. I had never heard of the political organization her family had dedicated their lives to, and I had certainly never been to the modern republic of Armenia. I had never even heard of the disputed Armenian lands of Nagorno and Karabakh or Soghomon Tehlirian, the Armenian revered by her kin for his assassination of Talaat Pasha in 1921 on a Berlin street. Pasha was one of the Turkish masterminds responsible for ordering the extermination of the Armenians in Turkey in 1915. His murder had been a cause for great celebration among Armenians throughout the world.

As a result of coming to know Taline and many others of my Armenian clients, I began to listen to Armenian music and read books by Chris Bogosian, Peter Balakian, and every book I could get my hands on about the genocide. The horror stories of the heads of Armenian intellectuals severed and displayed on posts in the middle of town squares or pregnant women whose babies had been cut from their wombs repulsed me. I began to watch the parade of Armenians coming in and out of Urartu across the street with greater interest and curiosity.

I couldn't help but notice the mirror that Taline inadvertently held up to my own life. Influenced by the feminist movement of the 1960s and 1970s, I had vowed never to marry a traditional man who didn't respect women. Though my parents were relatively modern in many ways, my front-row view of traditional marriage didn't fit the egalitarian mores that had begun sweeping the country and my psyche.

My mother had grown up in Albany, New York, the only daughter of Armenian immigrants and genocide survivors. Though she had managed to convince her "old country parents" to let her attend an American high school and college and had worked briefly as a social worker after graduating, once she met and married my father, he had considered it unacceptable for her to work outside the home. Instead, she devoted her considerable energy and intelligence to cooking gourmet meals, keeping an impossibly clean and orderly home, and ensuring that the four of us kids were always well-dressed, well-spoken, and exemplary in every way. Whenever my dad was home for dinner, she'd spend hours preparing Armenian meals of rice pilaf, stuffed peppers, grape leaves, and baklava, trying hard to please his expansive palette.

Over the years, I became accustomed to Mom's dinnertime ritual. As she hurried around the kitchen bringing the steaming dishes to the table, I set the table and called Dad in from his study to dinner. He was adamant about not being called before "everything was on the table." The five of us would then wait for Dad to sit down in his chair at the head of the table before we sat down. Mom would stand and dish out the various offerings, first serving my father, then my oldest brother, then my second brother, then my older sister, and finally, me and herself last. She ate only after completing this pecking order, jumping up and down throughout the meal to replenish the pilaf, fetch more green beans, or put out plates for the dessert. In many ways, this ritual epitomized for me a woman's place in the traditional Armenian family. Though Mom might have disagreed with me, it looked like she had gotten the poor end of the proverbial stick in that family pecking order.

I understood that Taline was caught between the old Armenian world of my grandparents and the new American world that Erica represented. Whatever she chose, something would be lost, and something would be gained. I empathized with her and wondered if she was so different from me. Weren't we both caught between these two worlds, trying to figure out where to land and where we fit in? While I initially believed us to be different, I saw that we both struggled with the same dilemma, just from different angles.

Taline struggled to integrate Southern California's modern American world with her parents' traditional Armenian world. I struggled to bring the rich history of my ancestors and grandparents into my modern American world. We seemed perfect complements to one another. In contrast to Taline's family who lived in a wholly Armenian world dedicated to the memory of the genocide and their cultural roots, spoke mainly Armenian with their friends and family, and socialized primarily with other Armenians, my family never spoke of the genocide, rarely spoke Armenian around us, and had chosen to assimilate wholly into the modern American culture.

Taline and my many other Armenian clients opened up portals to worlds I might never have known concerning my culture and ancestors.

Chapter 8

Struck by Lightning

The sun sat high in the sky on that bright July day in 2007 during our first journey to the Sacred Valley of Peru. Our tribe of about twenty-five sat in a circle on the hard, dry ground of the Peruvian mesa at upwards of 12,000 feet. Nary a tree in sight. The smell of burnt earth and drying twigs permeated the air. Men and women of all ages, including my husband Jim and our fifteen-year-old daughter Alicia, sat cross-legged or leaned against sagging backpacks. Sweat dripped down our streaked cheeks; discarded outer layers of clothing in every shape and color littered the ground. Wide-brimmed leather and cotton bucket hats shielded us from the scorching rays.

One by one, each of us raised ourselves from the parched earth and walked to the center of the circle. Pasquale, Francisco, and Vilma, the Peruvian shamans who had accompanied us up the long winding bus ride to the mountaintop, took turns cleansing our energy fields. The rest of us held sacred space, witnessing the ritual ceremonies.

Each shaman, dressed in intricately beaded red wool caps and long embroidered red ponchos, held their medicine bundles, called "mesas," high above our heads. The bundles, often weighing upwards of five pounds, and wrapped in brightly woven square tapestries, consisted of sacred stones, feathers, and artifacts gathered from the land and blessed by the healers. During the ceremony, each shaman, after holding her bundle high over our heads, mumbled blessings in Quechua, begging Spirit to "hampu hampu" or enter our souls and energy bodies and release whatever toxic energy no longer served us. They then knocked the medicine bundles hard over our heads, hearts, and solar plexuses, releasing whatever energy was ready to be removed. Finally, they waved their medicine bundles over our entire bodies, from head to toe, front and back, clearing and cleansing our energy fields while mumbling in Quechua. Each ritual cleansing took anywhere from three to five minutes.

I sat gazing into the distance as the individual cleansings proceeded, leaning against my backpack while the rocks of the earth bit into my skin. I felt bored and uncomfortable and wished only to return to the air-conditioned bus that would carry us back to civilization.

We'd been sitting for at least an hour when Vilma, diminutive but fierce, took her place alone in the center of the circle. Long black braids trailed down her back, tied in red ribbons at the ends. She must have been about 26 then. She wore her customary knee-length, native woven red-and-black wool skirt despite the 95-degree weather, accessorized by an embroidered white shirt, a mahogany calfskin wide-brimmed hat, and open-toed, black rubber sandals. A jagged scar stretched from high on her right cheekbone to the right side of her lip, causing her mouth to be crooked even when not smiling.

Suddenly, Vilma raised her right hand high, shaking her etched oblong gourd filled with dried seeds. A jet-black condor, wingspan seeming to stretch at least eleven feet, soared in circles directly above us as if trying to communicate. Vilma crooked her chin toward the condor and spoke quickly in Quechua. Whispers flew around the circle. Had she called in the condor, the sacred bird of the Andes? Was this an auspicious sign? All eyes turned heavenward to follow its wings as it circled high above us.

In Andean mythology, the condor rules over the upper world of the spirits and mediates between that upper world and the earthly world. It symbolizes power and health, life and rebirth, and is thought to carry the souls of the dead to the upper world on its massive wingspan.

I stared upward, enervated by the heat, not knowing what to think or feel, and watched, feeling as if something important was happening. I just wasn't sure what.

Lightning had struck Vilma's cheek at age seven while she was hiking in the mountains behind her village with her father. It was her third lightning strike. The first hit her while in the womb. The strike had knocked her mother unconscious, and the villagers assumed she and her mother had died. When her mother regained consciousness, the elders and curanderos gathered around, shaking their homemade rattles and prized condor feathers around her, begging the souls of Vilma and her mother to return to their bodies.

The second strike occurred during Vilma's birth at her family home. The surrounding families became suspicious, believing that the family must be hiding gold and silver, as lightning was thought only to strike the homes carrying such riches. But, Vilma told me later, there was no gold or silver in her home, just the knowledge on the part of her family that this new child, first struck by lightning in the womb and now upon her birth, would be a healer and a seer, as was ordained by the beliefs of the elders and curanderos.

While Vilma's lightning strikes had been literal, the ones that struck our little family of three in the fifteen years before that first trip to Peru had been more metaphorical.

———————

I remember standing near a grassy knoll overlooking the ocean just south of Santa Barbara. Jim and I had brought Mom and Dad to this little inn for a weekend respite. It was 1992, three years after a massive stroke left my seventy-seven-year-old father, still working at his lifelong ob-gyn practice, paralyzed on his left side, unable to speak, and wheelchair-bound. My mother, always dutiful, had remained by his side continually during the three months he lay immobilized in the hospital and in the years since. She was exhausted by the endless mundane tasks of keeping my father alive. Her knees buckled from lifting him in and out of his wheelchair, and she often snapped out of fatigue and frustration at anyone in her path. She spent her days ferrying Dad to and from neurologists, physical therapists, and cardiologists. She seemed on the verge of a breakdown.

I had parked Dad's wheelchair on the inn's small square of grass. Mom sat by him in a lawn chair, fussing with his lame foot and smoothing his thinning gray hair. The surf pounded the rocks below as the gulls circled above, and the smell of salt wafted through the air. Mom looked spent yet serene, content to sit idly by the shore.

I looked up toward the inn and saw Jim walk out onto its adjacent patio. He caught my eye and motioned gently with his right forefinger for me to join him. I walked up the hill from the cliff.

"Hey, I just got the results from the PET scan they did last week," he whispered so no one could hear.

I half-listened, my eyes focused on my parents. In my constant worrying about them, I hardly remembered Jim telling me he'd had any brain scans. Or maybe he hadn't told me at all.

"They say it's a kind of early dementia. They're not sure what kind. It may be Pick's disease. If so, I might only have a year to live."

I jolted out of my psychic fog.

"What? A year to live? What are you talking about?"

Jim was 39. He had taken a leave of absence from his thriving family medicine practice a year earlier when he began to forget small things, the names of favorite patients, the correct dosages of Prozac and Inderal, and meetings with colleagues. One day I opened the kitchen freezer to find a small, wooden-handled hoe sitting next to the ice cream.

What was a garden tool doing in the freezer?

That had shaken me. Thinking these symptoms were signs of stress and depression, Jim began seeing a psychiatrist and a psychologist. When, after a year, the symptoms persisted, he saw a neurologist.

We sat in the sterile beige office, Jim in one chair, Dr. Michael across from him, and I between them, forming a triangle. Dr. Michael's beige wooden desk, pushed against one wall, overflowed with charts and paperwork. No one spoke.

Dr. Michael pulled a sheet of blank white paper and a pencil from his desk and asked Jim to draw a cube. I watched with curiosity as Jim slowly drew the outline of a square, concentrating intently. He began to draw straight lines in random directions out from the square, unable to connect them or form the lines into any coherent shape. He handed the paper back to the doctor, who looked on dispassionately.

Dr. Michael then handed Jim another blank paper and asked him to draw the face of a clock with the numbers, minute hands, and second hand included. Jim carefully drew the circle. The twelve numbers he scribbled on the clock face occupied only one-half of the inside of the circle, were hardly legible, and were out of order. The clock hands were skewed in indecipherable directions.

Finally, he asked Jim to raise his right hand parallel to his nose and the right side of his face. "Now, bring your index finger toward your face and touch the tip of your nose."

Jim carefully dragged his finger toward his nose, firmly landing his hand on his collarbone, missing the nose completely. He tried repeatedly, but could not touch the tip of his nose with his right index finger.

I sat stunned, like the proverbial deer in the headlights, not knowing what to think. My gaze moved quizzically and anxiously between Jim and Dr. Michael, but neither spoke. Why couldn't he do these simple, basic things? What was happening here?

A week or so later, we sat in his psychiatrist's office in Westwood. "Jim," Brooke began, "I'm putting you out on disability."

She may have said more than that, but that's all I heard. My life as I knew it flashed before my eyes as if it was about to die.

———————

I had met Jim during my internship. He had recently finished his medical residency and was asked to stay on as an attending physician, teaching upcoming medical residents. The program incorporated medical and behavioral health, teaching the residents to work with psychologists to treat their patients.

He was funny and cute, with a boyish shock of dirty blonde hair and sparkly hazel eyes. I had been attracted not only by his broad smile and easy manner, but by the care and compassion he seemed to show everyone he met: the patients, the staff, the medical residents, and yes, even the behavioral health team. Our easy banter about the challenging patients of the day, the medical and psychological crises we encountered, and the general life of a healing professional drew me to him. I cherished our shared interest in the healing arts and the many levels on which we could share our experiences.

Now, I looked at Brooke and said curtly, "Do you know what you're saying?"

"Yeah," she replied. "I know exactly what I'm saying."

I sat stunned, contemplating what this meant for the life I had known, unable to fathom Jim not working again and we no longer sharing a common path as healing professionals.

Along with this realization came the fear that the dementia might progress. Lightning seemed to have struck not only Jim's life but life as we had experienced it in our seven years of marriage.

Thankfully, Jim didn't die that year, but doctors never determined either the cause or the exact nature of his unusually early dementia. He never practiced Western medicine again and spent the next fourteen years hanging around the house, gardening, taking care of our daughter Alicia, and feeding the menagerie of cats, dogs, ducks, chickens, and even donkeys living in our backyard. In his words, he lay "fallow" during that time, resting after his many arduous years of medical school, residency, and work as a teaching and private practice physician.

While I was grateful to have someone to walk our daughter to school every day and to pick her up every afternoon, I missed the days when we would come home after a long day's work and share our interesting experiences. And often, I felt resentful that Jim got to take Alicia to the park after school and attend the school picnics. By default, he became the primary caregiver without our ever having discussed it. I felt gratitude that he was still alive, but not without that occasional resentment, mixed with a healthy dose of powerlessness, over this peculiar lightning that had altered our lives.

Fourteen years after "retiring" from medicine, Jim got a call from our brother-in-law Terry.

"Hey, I'm going to Esalen next week. Wanna come with me and hear about shamanism? The speaker is supposed to be good and has written a ton of books."

"Nope. Not interested," said Jim, in his characteristic way. "But I'd love to soak in the hot tubs while you attend the conference."

Esalen sits perched on the Big Sur Coast overlooking the ocean. Known for its natural hot springs piped into stone baths on the cliff overlooking the ocean, it was a favorite getaway for both of us, offering psychology, yoga, and spirituality conferences in a stunningly beautiful setting.

"You have to register for the conference," Terry said.

"Ok, I'll register, but I doubt I'll go to the conference with you."

During one of the weekend sessions, Jim decided to walk with Terry to the big white tent perched on the edge of the lawn overlooking the Pacific. He listened for a few minutes to what the Cuban-American psychologist had to say about his 25 years living with curanderos in the mountains and jungles of South America. After about a half hour, Jim had heard enough and attempted to sneak out of the tent unnoticed and make his way back to the hot tubs. As he got up to leave, Alberto, the psychologist, asked for a volunteer. Jim sped toward the exit, head down, not looking back.

"Hey, you in the back, come on up here," Alberto called.

Jim looked around and found hundreds of eyes upon him.

"Me," he said sheepishly.

"Yeah, you. Come on up here."

Oh shit, thought Jim. *He caught me.* But ever the dutiful student, he made his way up to the front of the tent.

Alberto, a tall, thin graying man in his 50s, looked like a modern-day Indiana Jones in his khaki pants, wide-brimmed khaki hat, blue linen shirt, and khaki vest. He asked Jim to stand holding his arms straight out in front, with his hands clasped.

"Now, as I press down on your arms, resist me," coached Alberto.

Jim's outstretched arms hardly moved as Alberto tapped down upon them forcefully. Alberto then moved toward Jim's solar plexus, waving his right hand in a circular motion around Jim's midsection.

"Now, hold out your arms and resist me again." Almost immediately, Jim's arms swooped, still clasped, down toward his thighs, wholly weakened.

Jim stood dazed and unsure of what had happened. Alberto quickly moved his hands around Jim's solar plexus again, restoring his energy, and told him he could sit down. Whether intended or not, Alberto had gotten Jim's attention.

Jim spent the rest of that weekend in the big white tent, watching and listening. His gift as a healer became evident to Alberto early on, and he invited Jim to train and teach with him at his Four Winds Society soon after their first meeting. Jim continued studying energy medicine and shamanism in South America for many years, often with Alicia and me studying right alongside him.

He would go on to rebirth not only his health and his work as a healer but my life and Alicia's as well. Like the condor and Vilma, he and I would learn to mediate between this world and the world of the spirits, living in that mandorla between them.

Looking back with my own condor eyes, viewing this vast landscape from above, I see that Jim's dementia diagnosis and the experience of meeting Alberto at Esalen proved to be the metaphorical "lightning strikes" that changed the course of our lives forever.

Jim's illness led him to die to the life he once knew and set him on the road to becoming the medicine man he was meant to be, rather than the man of medicine he had thought he was supposed to be.

Chapter 9

Grandmother Jemela

Jake, my brother Jim's youngest son, texted one day, asking if I had ever heard of the psychiatrist Brian Weiss. "Of course," I responded. I had read his books on reincarnation and past life regression decades before when they were first published.

"Did you want to go to a workshop with him?" Jake asked. Thrilled to be invited to do anything with one of my hip, handsome young nephews, I readily agreed, particularly as I had often considered attending one of Brian Weiss' workshops. An entourage of family members showed up at the Pasadena Civic Auditorium that Saturday morning to support Jake, curious to see what would happen.

After a brief introduction, Dr. Weiss began to lead us through a past life regression. "Sit with your eyes closed and feet flat on the floor," Dr. Weiss' sonorous voice began. "I'm going to count very slowly down from ten to one. When I reach one, you will see a door before you. Ten, nine, eight, seven, six, five, four, three, two, one. Now you see the door. Open the door and step inside."

I stepped into the pale blue sky and fell into a cloudy, grey mist, tumbling to the ground. If I could have heard anything, I would have heard the thud I made when I reached the bottom, but I heard nothing.

"Look at the ground beneath you. Look around you. What do you see? What are you wearing, and who is there with you?"

As I look down, I see that I am standing alone in a short narrow hallway with sparkling hardwood floors and unadorned white walls. I gaze down at the leather lace-up shoes on my feet, the very picture of "sensible." I am wearing thick, beige opaque stockings and an old-fashioned flowered shirt-waist dress bowed at the waist on a stout body. As I look down the hall-way, I see a screen door opening into a small barren dirt yard. I feel very alone, even though a wizened older man sits quietly, smoking a cigar and rocking in his chair, in the corner of the room behind me. I recognize the man as my paternal grandfather.

I am sick, very sick. I have been told I have ovarian cancer and will die soon. I am not afraid of death. I welcome its relief from this life. My two children are grown now with their own children and have very little time for me. I have nothing more to say to the man in the corner whom I was forced to marry more than forty-three years ago. I feel ready to die.

I was shocked out of my reverie and back into the packed auditorium when I heard Dr. Weiss' voice again. Shaken by what I experienced, I blinked and looked around the crowded, brightly lit room. I stamped my feet on the ground to feel its solidity. I saw Jim sitting beside me and my brother Jim, his wife Cindy, and Jake behind me. I realized that I had entered the life of my grandmother Jemela who died the year before I was born and after whom I am named. I was surprised to feel her loneliness and embrace of the death that apparently traumatized my parents.

I thought back on an incident many years previous when my jokester sister Lynne had laughingly asked my staunchly Christian father if he thought that I might be the reincarnation of his mother. Out of the fog of his stroke, my stoic father had gently nodded his head and uttered a muffled "maybe."

Grandmother Jemela died at age 63, the age I am now as I write this, devastating my father, her only son. My mother described how my father, a gynecological surgeon, had opened up his mother's uterus for exploratory surgery, only to find it riddled with cancer too advanced to treat. Overcome with the guilt of not having caught the cancer sooner, my father fell into a depression and disappeared for three days after his mother's death, so great was his grief.

Grandmother Jemela was born in 1891, one of five children in Aintab. Family lore says that an employee of my great-grandfather had warned him "The Turks are coming to get you," prompting him to flee south with his family sometime before the genocide. I have no idea exactly what year they fled or who that "employee" might have been.

I've heard two stories of how Grandmother Jemela made it out of Turkey to New York. The first paints a picture of the family en route from Aintab to the refugee camps in Aleppo, Syria, passing a Turkish port where a vessel headed to New York lay moored. Desperate to save the life of his children, my great-grandfather booked passage for his three daughters, Jemela, Mary, and Victoria, on the boat to America and safety. He then continued to Aleppo with his two sons.

The second, more plausible story has twenty-year-old Grandmother Jemela sent to America directly from Aintab sometime in 1911 to marry her betrothed, a shoemaker very much her senior, whom she hardly knew. The shoemaker, Armen Mahsereghian, had been making Jemela's shoes for years and had "fallen in love with her feet." He had escaped to America and written asking for Jemela's hand in marriage. Jemela, however, was in love with a "Lusavorchegan," an Armenian Orthodox boy in Aintab. Her parents forbade her to marry the boy due to religious differences, as her family worshiped in the Protestant Armenian church. So in that story, Jemela was shipped off to New York with a couple of close girlfriends to marry Armen.

Grandmother Jemela arrived on Ellis Island sometime around 1911 and was immediately married there, as was the custom, before being permitted to enter the mainland. My father, George, was born a year later in New York City in 1912, and my Aunty Gladys four years later. It would be several years before my grandparents, my dad, and my aunt would board a train west to California to set up a new cobbler's shop and life in Pasadena.

When I think back over the experience of the past life regression in which I stepped into the life of my grandmother, emotions of curiosity, pride, and sadness swirl together with this question: What might it mean to have been my father's mother in a previous life?

Throughout my life, I have felt a distinct love and protectiveness toward my father and his extended family, particularly his younger sister, Aunty Gladys, and his first cousin, Johno. My heart has swelled with love toward them in a way quite different from the more distant feelings I have carried for my mother's family. To the extent that my mother's fierce lioness personality often scared and pushed me away, my father's cuddly brown teddy-bear ways always pulled me in for an embrace. The regression explained this particular love that I held for my father and his family. If I had been my father's mother in a previous life, wouldn't I naturally feel a special love for him and his family?

Some say that families reincarnate in soul groups, coming back life after life to assume different roles in each other's lives. Had I returned as my father's daughter to spend more time with him and my aunt? It made sense to me.

I also felt pride that I might have been my dad's mother. To me, Dad was the most beloved in our family. It felt an honor to have been his mother. I understood her as strong, capable, and respected. In a family where I sometimes felt overlooked, becoming *her* gave me a value I coveted.

Had I conjured up this regression as a salve for the bruised ego of a child who sometimes felt invisible? Was this regression my way of saying, "See, I'm someone special after all?"

It's hard to know.

To my eye, though, Grandma Jemela was also unattractive. From the few pictures I'd seen, she looked thick and square, dressed dowdily in homemade cotton shirt dresses, with a bulbous Armenian nose, round, horn-rimmed glasses, and a face scarred with acne. I often asked Aunty Gladys if Grandmother Jemela was fat.

"No, dear," she would reply, "just a size 16, always a size 16."

Size 16. That was fat in my book and not dissimilar to the size I always struggled to shrink.

So when one of my brothers told me I looked like her, I burned with shame and embarrassment. She had been no beauty, and it hurt that they likened me to her. I was proud to have been her but ashamed to look like her.

Maybe though, Grandma Jemela was not ashamed to look as she did. Perhaps she accepted parts of herself that I had rejected. Maybe I had a lot to learn from her regarding self-love and acceptance. Perhaps she had grown up in a time and place when women weren't judged by the size of their bodies but rather by the qualities of their character. Entertaining this notion proved comforting and healing to me.

———————

Returning in my mind's eye to the regression, I thought of the older man, Grandmother Jemela's husband, my grandfather, sitting in the corner of the living room, rocking and smoking. I felt Grandmother Jemela's loneliness and disconnection from this man she never wanted to marry. I felt sad for her loneliness and sorry that she had arrived at a place in her life where she no longer wanted to continue. In the flash of those few moments, I experienced the expanse of a life I had known little about.

What struck me most strongly about the regression was Grandmother Jemela's acceptance of her death. We are physicians and healers in my family. To want to die of the ovarian cancer, which my parents and aunt considered a tragedy, unbalanced me and shed new light on what my grandmother's life must have been like.

The regression provided me with a new view of death as something to be embraced rather than feared. It is taboo in many American families, including mine, to accept death, particularly at a relatively young age. When a stroke paralyzed my father at 77, he fought hard for 13 years to regain his speech and re-learn to walk. He told no one of his desire to die except my husband, whom he begged not to speak about this desire until his death. In many families, we aren't allowed to welcome death. Our job is to live. For that reason, residing in my grandmother's body and feeling her willingness to die continues to shake me. At the same time, I felt a kind of relief for her. To her, maybe her death wasn't a tragedy at all but a blessing, a welcomed moving on.

Shamans believe that by healing ourselves, we heal generations of ancestors past and generations yet to be born. In my life, I have had the great luxury of choosing differently from the prescribed roles of my mother and grandmother. Have I freed them to live a different life than the one thrust upon them? And what have I passed on to my daughter?

These questions swirl within me.

I reflect on the shamanic journey I took many years ago with Jim in the Grand Canyon, when I heard Grandmother Jemela's voice saying, "Heal me. Live the life I could not live." What does it mean to heal another by the very act of living one's own life? I had so many choices, so many options. Hers were limited. She was sent to a new country to marry a man she had only known as her shoemaker and, like my own mother, she was not allowed to work outside the home. I had choices at so many junctures: where to go to college, what to study, whom to marry, what career to follow, where to live, and how to live.

I ask Grandmother Jemela silently, have I lived the life you could not live? Have I made the most of the choices and options available to me? Have I adequately honored your exhortation to me so many years ago?

I hope so. I am grateful to Grandmother Jemela for the struggles she endured so I could have the life I now live.

Chapter 10

Michelle and the Family Constellation

"Hey, my doctor recommended I do something called a Family Constellation to deal with family issues," my friend Kim said one night as we sipped a glass of wine on my front porch. "Have you ever heard of that?"

"Sure," I replied. "I know something about Family Constellations. Not a lot. But something." Started by the German psychotherapist Burt Hellinger in the mid-1990s, I knew it was a therapeutic modality where members of a small group stand in for the family members of the person presenting with an issue, with the aim of bringing to light unconscious family dynamics that the person might be carrying. I had seen it in action when one of my clients asked me to accompany her to a Family Constellation session a few months earlier, facilitated by the same woman to whom Kim was referred. I found it fascinating and was eager to witness it again.

"Want me to go along with you?" There was some part of me that very much wanted to accompany Kim. We had been best friends for fifty years, and I valued her healing as much as I valued my own, but my enthusiasm seemed more than that. I didn't realize why at the time.

On the evening of the Family Constellation session, we arrived at the square brick Altadena Healing Center at 6:45 to prepare for the 7

p.m. session. Deep, cushioned chairs nestled against the walls of a sizeable space, thickly carpeted in soft beige hues. Eight or ten people I
didn't recognize occupied the chairs. Homey plaques with inspirational
sayings painted in earth tones decorated the walls, giving the place a
warm ambiance. We took our seats across the room from Elisabeth,
the facilitator, a plain, blond woman in her 40s who spoke with a German accent.

Elisabeth facilitated two sessions every Thursday evening in this
Altadena center, a mere fifteen-minute drive from my La Canada home
and just down the street from where I grew up.

Kim's was the first constellation session scheduled for that night.
Halfway through her session, I sensed that the second person slated to
work that evening wasn't in the room. I pondered whether to volunteer. Sure enough, when it came time to begin the second Family Constellation, Elisabeth announced that the second person scheduled for
that night wasn't coming. Did anyone want to take her place?

My hand shot up, almost involuntarily.

"What would you like to work with?" Elisabeth asked.

"Depression," I replied, almost without thinking.

Elisabeth began by asking me a bit about my depression and my
family history. I said I was Armenian, and she seemed familiar with the
events of the genocide, which surprised me. Elisabeth then picked
characters from the individuals sitting around the room to represent
Mom, Dad, Me, and Depression. She also selected people to represent
two of my unnamed deceased ancestors. The actors were to intuitively
and energetically act out my family dynamics and any traumas passed
down unconsciously from one generation to the next. I observed silently from the sidelines.

Quickly, the six characters spread out throughout the room.

Almost immediately, the character playing Mom moved away from
the character playing Me, her attention focused wholly on herself. Dad
stood behind me, also turned away, involved in something deep within
himself.

Depression wrapped her arms around me as if enamored, playing
with my hair and gently stroking my face.

My stomach knotted as I watched. I didn't like Depression embracing me. I wanted her to get away, to unwrap her tendrils and flee.
I noted the distance between my character and those of Mom and Dad,
each looking wrapped in their individual reveries. I was struck by their

lack of interaction with the character playing Me, leaving Me alone in the middle of the room with Depression.

Suddenly Elisabeth spoke: "What happened to your mother?"

"I don't know," I responded, but mentioned that there had been vague talk of abuse when my mother was a child. I also said that Mom had been the daughter of two Armenian Genocide survivors.

"There is betrayal in the room," Elisabeth said. "Your mother could not focus on or see you because of this unspoken trauma. There's a good chance that the abuse had been passed down from generation to generation."

I listened silently, intrigued, taking in the information.

"Abuse and betrayal. Your mother unconsciously projected both onto you. You carried her trauma so your mother did not have to carry it alone."

This resonated deeply. I felt a sense of relief at understanding some of my lifelong mild depression, but also sad. Sad for Mom and sad for me.

Soon, Depression left me and wrapped herself around Dad. I became angry watching Me watch Dad, both of us looking helpless. I wanted Depression to leave him alone. I didn't want Dad to be entangled with Depression. I wanted it to leave all of us alone.

Elisabeth then asked the characters depicting Mom and Dad to stand beside each other. The healthy male and female ancestors took their places, standing behind Mom and Dad and supporting them. Depression moved to a corner of the room. Elisabeth then asked Me to stand before the newly positioned Mom and Dad.

I felt a sense of strength as I watched Me stand firmly before the solid presence of my parents and their healthy ancestors. I felt supported by and allied with my parents.

"Now give the depression back to your parents. It does not belong to you. It belongs to them," said Elisabeth. "Say this to your parents and your ancestors: I give the depression back to you. It is not mine. It does not belong to me. It belongs to you. I was too little to take it on, and it has been too much for me to carry."

I wondered about the veracity of the last statement. I had carried the depression for many decades. I had wanted to spare them pain. I wasn't sure I was ready to return it to them now.

I repeated the words to Mom and Dad nonetheless. "I give the depression back to you. It is not mine. It does not belong to me. It belongs to you. I was too little to take it on, and it has been too much for me to carry."

Mom and Dad willingly took back the depression, leaving me momentarily freed from it, and Depression went to stand beside them. I felt lighter and freer. But I gave the depression back reluctantly, not wanting to burden further these parents whom I loved so much.

As the players returned to their seats and the Family Constellation dismantled, I made a silent vow to myself to try healing whatever remained of Depression with me so as not to further pass it on to Alicia.

––––––––––––––

About a year and a half after the Family Constellation session, Jim gifted me a phone session with one of his clients, Michelle, an energy practitioner and healer. Having heard about Michelle and taken some of her online classes, I respected her and her work and answered the phone eagerly and anxiously.

"So, tell me about the trauma," Michelle began suddenly, curtly.

Well, that's not much of a "hello," I thought.

"Uh, trauma?" I answered, a little stunned at her sudden dive in. "Well, I, um, well, I don't know if I've had much trauma."

"Yes, you have," she retorted.

"Well, there was some yelling growing up, but I don't know if that counts as trauma."

"That's not it."

I reeled back, knocked off my equilibrium by her certainty.

"Ahh," she continued thoughtfully, "perhaps it was your mother's trauma you took on."

"Uh, well, maybe. I don't know."

"What trauma did your mother experience?"

"Well, there was some talk of her being abused as a child, but I don't know much about it. My sister mentioned it once."

"That sounds about right. Did her father abuse her?"

"I don't think so. I think it was an uncle or someone who lived downstairs, but I'm not sure."

"It was her father," Michelle stated matter-of-factly.

How was she so sure? I wondered. But I was reminded of the Family Constellation session the year before. I was also disturbed that my seemingly kind and generous grandfather might have somehow hurt my mother. Very disturbed. No part of me wanted to believe it, and to this day, I'm not sure I do.

Michelle went on to say that my maternal grandfather, Hagop, who'd walked out of Turkey at age 19 alone to escape the genocide, had been possessed of dark energies from the trauma of being forced to leave his family and homeland. He'd projected his darkness onto my mother as a child, taking advantage of her innocence, passing on the horror and rage he couldn't personally acknowledge.

"You believed it was your job to remove your mother's pain," continued Michelle. "You came into this life to do that. You stopped her from her path of healing. She didn't go down her own road. You had no boundaries as a child and took it on for her. I wish you'd had better boundaries for her and yourself."

Better boundaries? I was offended. How on earth could I have known to erect better boundaries as a child? But I sat pensively, considering her statements. Much of what Michelle said resonated in some deep part of me, as it had with Elisabeth the year before. Not my mother's abuse by her father, but the projection of darkness onto Mom by her father and then onto me.

My maternal grandfather had been a tall man with an ever-present smile and twinkling blue eyes. After immigrating to the States, he worked his way up from being a butcher in a small New York shop to owning a chain of Grand Cash grocery stores in Albany, New York. When we visited, he'd set us loose in his stores, exclaiming, "Take whatever you want." I had felt, literally, like the kid in the candy store and often walked out with handfuls of Butterfingers and Junior Mints. When he'd visited us in California, his common refrain to the four kids was "Let me shaka your hand, honey," in his thick Armenian accent. He'd take our small hand in his much larger one, leaving within it a crisp, new twenty-dollar bill or a large check at holidays.

It was hard to reconcile this ebullient man with the "dark energies" Michelle mentioned, but on some levels, it made sense.

In my mind, I saw the line of trauma passed down from my maternal grandfather, a genocide survivor, to my mother, to myself. I knew that from the earliest age, I had tried to heal my mother's pain, the pain she denied having but exhibited daily in her sometimes anxious behavior. I mollified her and did anything I could to make her happy. It never occurred to me that she carried the pain of her jolly, seemingly happy father and her tiny, silent mother. Given how painful I imagined his life had been, I'd always wondered how he could appear so happy.

Perhaps he wasn't, I thought, for the first time.

———————

Armenians carry within them a leaded vein of melancholy. I've learned this after many years of living and working with Armenian people and writing my doctoral dissertation about them. The depression of the oppression of an ancient battered tribe, buffeted by the surrounding powers of Russia and Iran and Turkey, a throughway to other places to be conquered. Nobody ever mentioned to me the depression coursing through the veins of my people. I discovered it for myself.

Do they, do we, know this about ourselves? Why didn't anyone tell me?

The genocide cuts a huge narcissistic gash in the soul of Armenians, a cut so deep that some are left with bleeding that never stops and spills over into everything they do. Others, like my parents and grandparents, defended mightily against that wound, blocking it with achievement, success, and persistent activity.

I remember a conversation I had with my ninety-four-year-old mother a few years before her death. Suffering from dementia, sitting alone in the big, window-framed living room of my sister's home, she looked at me beseechingly and asked, with tears in her eyes, "What have I done, Jemela? Why does everyone hate me? Why doesn't anyone love me anymore? Why don't they come to visit me?"

My heart seized as I tried to comfort her.

"Mom, you didn't do anything. You've just outlived all your friends and your family and Dad." The dementia seemed to open up in her a deep wound of feeling unwanted and unloved. But I wondered if this pain, seemingly born of the forgetfulness of dementia, didn't speak to a more profound ancestral fear.

Why do they hate us? Why have they driven us from our homes, left us alone, and killed us? What have we done to deserve this?

SECTION TWO

The Genocide Tour

In the summer of 2015, I was 59 and responding to an inner call to learn more about my ancestral origins. I embarked on a two-week tour of ancient Western Armenia, now situated in present-day Turkey. I longed to visit the birthplaces of my four Armenian grandparents, and learn firsthand about the country from which they fled.

On that journey, which I came to call "The Genocide Tour," I faced a silenced, traumatic part of my family history. After returning home from the tour, deceased ancestral spirits haunted my days and nights, and I was forced to face my own inner trauma.

The Genocide Tour became formative in my understanding of myself as an Armenian-American and began the healing and integration of my ancestral soul.

Map of Turkey

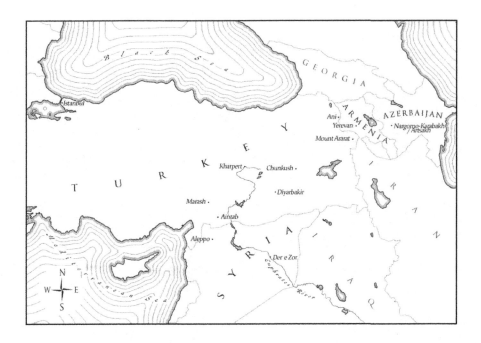

Chapter 11

Istanbul

Istanbul: gateway to the East, Byzantium, the Bosporus, Hagia Sofia, Constantinople. The very word created tingles of anticipation up and down my spine. I envisioned bearded men smoking hookahs in the cobbled, narrow streets of the Grand Bazaar, gold-laden caftans hanging from mud rafters, baklava brimming with pistachios and dripping honey on every street corner, and the mournful call to prayer wafting from the minarets of the Blue Mosque. With my love of the exotic, I knew I would love Istanbul. I feared I might even want to move there, to the country of my ancestors.

I had heard that Sarkis, a friend of Aunty Gladys from her local Pasadena Armenian church, led Armenian pilgrims to Turkey, taking them to the birthplaces of their Armenian parents and grandparents. A seemingly kind man in his early 70s, slightly balding with a gentle yet serious demeanor, he had directed the church choir for years. I had seen him a time or two when visiting the church for funerals and fundraisers but had never actually spoken with him. He had led upwards of sixty or seventy of these pilgrimages to Turkey and apparently possessed a near-encyclopedic knowledge of all things Armenian.

Wow, I thought. Finally, a chance to experience Turkey's romance firsthand and visit the birthplaces of my four grandparents.

On his Facebook page, I read that Sarkis had a trip leaving in a few weeks. I reached out to him, asking if he had any openings.

"Would you be coming alone?" he asked.

I laughed and said yes. Jim had little interest in Turkey or anything Armenian, and my daughter was working in Big Sur for the summer, having just graduated from college. I doubted that my brothers would be interested, and my sister had traveled to our grandparents' hometowns years before.

"Yes," I answered. "I'll be coming alone."

"Great," he replied, "because we only have one seat left in the van."

Three of my four grandparents, including Grandmother Jemela, were born and raised in Aintab. Aintab had been part of the family vocabulary since my birth. I hadn't known until recently that my mother's father, Hacop, had come from a neighboring town, Marash.

"Is this tour going to Aintab and Marash?" I asked Sarkis.

"Yes."

Soon after I registered for the trip, brief, unbidden visions appeared to me in the night just before drifting off to sleep and on awakening in the morning. They seemed to want to tell me something. I just didn't know what.

In the first of the visions, a beautiful dark-skinned girl, about nine years old, stared mutely out at me, her black eyes shining, a white shawl draped over her mud-smudged hair in the Islamic fashion. I heard a word that sounded like "carport" ringing hazily over the scene. Having never heard the word, I pulled up a map of Turkey from my computer, searching for something akin to it. I noted a town called Kharpert on the map, located in Central Turkey. Consulting the itinerary for our trip, I saw that we would indeed be going to Kharpert. I had no idea what the vision meant or what the little girl intended to convey to me. Was she me in another incarnation? Had I known her? Had I, or one of my ancestors, once lived there? She haunted me, and I see her face to this day.

In another vision, I witnessed a younger girl of about five, alone, filthy, in rags, hiding in a barn. She was emaciated and standing upon a bed of dry ochre hay. Her hair lay in strings, matted and dirty, and she peered forlornly out of the barn door, frightened yet looking for something. Was she hiding from the Turkish soldiers rounding up Armenians and taking them to murder in the town square, or was she waiting for something else?

On a third night, I woke up with the word "darezore" on my mind. Another look at the map revealed the southern Syrian desert town of

Deir ez-Zor, where Armenian refugees arrived if they survived the death marches through southern Turkey into Syria. Had I heard of Deir ez-Zor and not remembered it, or was something else reaching into my consciousness at night, perhaps warning me of what was to come? Had I stepped back into another time and place in that liminal space between waking and dreaming? As with the previous visions, I had yet to learn what they meant.

I began to sense this tour wouldn't be a joyride through the romantic streets of Istanbul after all, but perhaps something more profound. I became fraught with apprehension and nerves, wondering if I was making the right decision to take the trip. But something led me on.

I flew alone from Los Angeles to Istanbul in July 2015, which coincidentally happened to be the 100th anniversary of the 1915 Armenian Genocide. I had no consciousness of the date's significance when I signed up for the trip. I realized it only after committing to it.

Istanbul lies on the westernmost edge of Turkey, hovering over the Bosporus Sea and straddling Europe and Asia. It's not only the largest city in Turkey but also the largest in Europe and serves as Turkey's cultural, economic, and historic center.

Upon arriving in Istanbul, after the eleven-hour flight, I checked into my upscale hotel in the new section of town and picked up a message to meet our tour group at a nearby restaurant. The trip coincided with the Islamic holy month of Ramadan, when observant Muslims fast from sunup to sundown. Turkey is an Islamic country, mainly composed of Sunni Muslims, and most of the Turkish people we met kept the fast.

On that first night, and every night after, I met our group of 17 in the designated restaurant full of Turkish people waiting to break the fast. We sat at long, white-clothed tables laden with plates of food: beef kebabs, spiced yogurt, rice pilaf, mounds of pita bread with onions and tomatoes, and small wheat and beef meatballs called "kufte." A glass of water stood by every place setting. As I sat down, I noticed no one eating, though the food was laid out and prepared. I greeted my fellow travelers and reached for a welcome sip of water after my long day of travel. One of the servers streaked toward me, yelling something incomprehensible in Turkish and waving his hands violently toward the glass in my hand. I sat startled, wide-eyed. What was happening?

Sarkis quickly said that we were not allowed water until the designated minute of sundown. The sun set at 8:17 that night. I put the glass down and coiled my hands in my lap. The group fell silent, staring at the food until the servers indicated eating was permitted.

Thus began the eating ritual that repeated every night of the trip, the only difference the particular town, the time of sunset, and the foods eaten. Our group comprised a motley array of Armenians from various parts of the world: a couple in their seventies from Beirut, with their sister and a friend; a forty-something actress from LA; the Sarafian family of six from Long Island with their 87-year-old friend Eleni; and an elderly couple originally from Syria and now living in South Pasadena. Sarkis and his incredibly competent, trilingual assistant, Arpi, rounded out the group.

By day, the seventeen of us crowded into a small, white Mercedes van. We traveled for long hours to the towns where our relatives lived before the 1915 genocide. Swirling tongues I couldn't understand danced around me: Turkish, Arabic, Armenian, everything it seemed except English. Though the Sarafians primarily spoke English, Seva and her husband spoke Armenian, and the four kids tended to keep to themselves at the back of the van. I felt locked in a self-imposed Tower of Babel, pressed against a side window peering out into the Turkish expanse.

Periodically the entire bus would burst out in Armenian song, startling me out of my internal reverie. How the hell did they all know the words to the same songs? The lack of a common language left me isolated in my mind. One of the older men looked at me suspiciously, querying in accented English why I was there. I didn't have an Armenian name, and I didn't speak Turkish or Armenian. He never seemed convinced that I was indeed Armenian and deserved to accompany him on this bus.

On our first outing in Istanbul, we visited the Balıklı Armenian Cemetery, a park-like oasis of green swaying trees and wide shaded avenues in the city's heart. The seventeen of us strolled past huge gray gravestones etched with charcoal-grey Armenian crosses. Praying angels adorned other headstones, along with the distinctive curves of the familiar, yet incompressible to me, Armenian script.

Sarkis stopped in front of a gravesite more ornate than the others. A three-dimensional black marble bust of a middle-aged man's head covered with wavy curls sat atop a tall white marble pillar. White marble doves attached to the pillar faced inward toward the sculpture. Angels peered down from an even taller marble plank placed behind the sculpted face. In front of the shrine, a tiny marble cherub sat cross-legged on the ground, staring up at us.

This grave lacked any Armenian script, as if we should know its occupant by its appearance. Someone had left a large 12" by 12" photo of a handsome middle-aged man at the base of the shrine. His visage mirrored that of the black marble bust. Flowers were scattered throughout the site.

Sarkis explained that the sculpted face represented Hrant Dink, an Armenian activist and journalist gunned down outside his office in 2007 for having been critical of the Turkish government; he had "spoken out against Turkishness" in his periodical *Agos*. He had founded the journal as a vehicle for speaking out about the genocide and had worked hard to further Armenian-Turkish reconciliation in Istanbul. *Agos* was the only periodical in Turkey that was written and printed in both Turkish and Armenian.

My cousin Maral had mentioned the name Hrant Dink to me years before, but I had no memory of why and had been embarrassed to admit that I had never heard of him. Now I stood before his grave, gazing at the flowers strewn at the shrine's base, the little cherub peering up at me. As my gaze focused, I sensed blurs of what seemed like hundreds of opaque, white spirits swirling around the plot, swirling in circles, panicked, as if with nowhere to go, and weeping. Weeping for him or weeping for themselves?

A poignant sense of sadness permeated the air. We stood mutely around the grave, staring.

The swirling spirits unnerved me. I felt dizzy, moved away from the group, and looked away, willing the vision to disappear. I felt the pain, the admiration, and the love of these figures for this man. My stomach roiled. Was the heat of the July day taking its toll on me, had the food the night before nauseated me, or was there something about these spirits and this grave that had infiltrated my very being?

As the tour continued through the cemetery, I walked apart as if in a daze.

Later that day, we drove by the offices of the periodical *Agos*. A simple one-foot square bronze placard, etched only with the one word *Agos*, indicated the location of the offices, belying the importance of the periodical or the man.

After returning home, I read that on the day of Hrant Dink's funeral in January 2007, hundreds of thousands of Armenians and Turks marched together through the streets of Istanbul, protesting his senseless murder by a Turkish nationalist. The chant "We are all Hrant Dink" rang through the streets. Reflecting upon the visit later, I thought of the courage of this man, a husband and a father, who had received numerous death threats because he was speaking out about the Armenian Genocide. He nonetheless attempted a reconciliation between the Turks and the small Armenian community in Istanbul.

The story of Hrant Dink reminded me of the danger of being an Armenian in Turkey, even in the 21st century, and I shuddered.

Chapter 12

Aintab and Marash

After several days of visiting the few remnants of Armenian life left in Istanbul, our trip moved south and eastward into the Cilician plateau in central Turkey. Early in the journey, we visited Aintab.

Beautiful, pale-green limestone buildings lined the wide boulevards of the former Armenian section of what had become a modern city. We visited several Armenian churches and homesteads now turned into mosques and teahouses. As we passed each tall limestone building, Sarkis would tell us the name of its pre-genocide occupants: "The Nazarians lived here; this is the Karamazian home; here lived the Ashjians." I found many of the names familiar, having heard them mentioned by family members during my childhood. I imagined these long-deceased friends and relatives praying in the ancient churches, breaking lavash, and sipping iced yogurt around their family dinner tables.

I desperately tried to imagine Grandmother Jemela as a child running through the streets, braids flying, giggling with her girlfriends on the way to school, or standing in bakery lines buying bread for supper. What had her life been like here in this beautiful city? Had she been happy? Did she feel safe and loved? I could only imagine.

I also wondered what it must have been like to be ripped from the only home she'd ever known and sent to the new world. Was she scared? What beloved items might she have carried with her? How was the journey, and who went with her? So many questions, all unanswered.

As our group walked through the center of the Armenian section, we stopped at the former Surp Asdvadzadzin (Holy Virgin Mary) church, large enough to cover an entire city block and built in the characteristic lime and brown stone of early Armenian architecture. I had read that Armenian women and children had fled there to escape the Turkish gendarmes, believing a church might offer sanctuary. Perhaps, here too, as in many other Armenian churches throughout the land, the gendarmes locked the church doors, set it on fire, and left the inhabitants to burn to death. Though neither my mother nor my jovial, outgoing grandfather ever discussed it, my great-grandmother may have been one among them.

The Surp Asdvadzadzin church, like most Armenian churches in Turkey, had been turned into a mosque, this one named the Liberation Mosque, serving the Islamic population of Aintab, with all remnants of its Armenian history washed away. As I trudged from the vast edifice back to the van, I felt a leaden blanket of heaviness descend upon me.

We took a short trip from Aintab to the neighboring city of Marash. Two crumbling two-story buildings of dark wood still stood, the only remains of the previous Armenian sector of Marash. I stared at the abandoned, decaying shacks and tried, to no avail, to imagine my vivacious grandfather living in one of those rundown edifices. Where had the rest of this formerly Armenian town disappeared to? I could only assume that the rest of the town had been demolished during the genocide.

At every church-turned-mosque along the journey, Sarkis and Arpi pointed out hidden remnants of our Armenian heritage: a cross carved into the cornerstone of a limestone brick; a chiseled pomegranate, the Armenian symbol of fertility hidden in a cubicle; Armenian lettering scrawled onto a closet wall. With every step, it seemed as if the trip had become a search not only for the homeland of our ancestors but for a culture lost and destroyed. Both anger and sadness welled within me at how little remained of my culture in our centuries-old homeland.

Chapter 13

Kharpert, Chunkush, and the Dudan Crevasse

For several hours after leaving Marash, my maternal grandfather's hometown, our crew traveled northward. Finally, we inched up a winding road that snaked around a city perched high above the dry Anatolian plateau. I felt my heart flutter in anticipation of arriving at this city that had introduced itself to me in the nighttime vision of the young girl, face smudged with dirt, hair covered in a graying white shawl. Also, in that vision, I had seen a single, crumbling red-brick facade about two feet thick and forty feet high.

As our van approached the apex of the hill, I gasped. On the side of the mountain stood the red-brick wall from my vision—the solitary ruin perched perpendicular to the hillside, a sentry guarding the barren plain below. Four uneven gaps in the stone, like portals, opened from the top of the thick wall.

I trembled. After leaving the van, I wandered alone through the streets of Kharpert, dazed, trying to sense why I was there and what I was supposed to see. I don't remember if Sarkis told us anything about the city of Kharpert and why we had come there. I welcomed the solitude. Something about the town, the gentle, warm air, and clean, well-swept streets, seemed familiar. I ambled along the winding roads, gazing into houses and climbing through ruined, abandoned churches until Sarkis called us back to the van.

I wondered again why the town of Kharpert had come to me and about the young girl with the sad eyes. I closed my eyes and mentally returned to the vision to try to understand. I asked her why she had contacted me and what she wanted.

"I want you to know what happened here," I heard her tell me. "They took my family and friends, and now I am alone. We were a town of churches. Now they are all ruined, standing like orphans on the side of this hill." I wanted to ask her more, but she faded away. I felt the sadness stick in my belly and my throat like hardened resin. She had tried to tell me something. That's why she came to me. I tried to summon her back.

"Why here, why Kharpert?" I asked. But she gave me no answer.

Throughout the Genocide Tour, I had hoped to feel some kinship, some familiarity, and some sense of home in this country of my ancestors, particularly in Aintab and Marash. I had grown up around the Turkish language and with Turkish and Armenian food. I had expected to love Turkey. Instead, I had been revolted, nauseated by what had happened, and anxious to leave. In Kharpert, far from my grandparents' hometowns, I finally felt that sense of home and the familiarity I had been seeking. I can't tell you what the houses looked like or even if there were any trees on the barren hills. All I remember is the winding road to the top of the city, the many blown-out, orphaned, and ruined churches dotting the side of the hillside, and the sense of warmth and belonging I felt there.

Returning to the van after our few hours in Kharpert, I hid in one of the back seats as we left, silent and pensive. As my traveling mates chattered on in Armenian, the van slowly wound down the hill into the valley below. Why had Kharpert seemed so familiar to me? Had I been there before in some other incarnation, or was it familiar from my vision? Again, I didn't know the answers to my questions, but Kharpert, of all the towns we visited that summer, left an imprint on my heart.

After a forty-five-minute drive from Kharpert, we stopped in an arid desert, dead tumbleweeds dotting the horizon. Leaving the van, we sidled up to a vast natural ravine burrowed deep into the ground. Grey-blue boulders of all sizes and shapes formed a perimeter around the gorge and sank into a ditch hundreds of feet deep and maybe a hundred feet wide. No houses, people, or life at all existed around the ravine, just grey and white boulders strewn throughout the canyon like an army of fallen soldiers. This was the Dudan Crevasse.

Our group stood at the side of the gorge, peering in. Sarkis explained that in 1915, the 10,000 residents of the neighboring town of Chunkush, all Armenians, had been marched to this gorge, tied in bundles of eight to ten, and thrown into the Crevasse, often while simultaneously shot or bayoneted. Their mangled bodies were left there to rot.

My stomach lurched, trying to imagine the horrific scene. I didn't know how to take in this information. My body felt frozen as I gazed into the long, deep canyon.

On the tour, I had struck up an unlikely companionship with Eleni, the 87-year-old real estate agent from Long Island. Eleni and I were two of the three single outliers in this caravan of couples and families. The family of six, friends from her Armenian church in New York, had invited Eleni to join them on the tour, but they stuck largely together, leaving Eleni on her own. I had hoped to befriend the one other single woman on our trip, the actress from LA in her late forties, but she befriended Sarkis, our guide, sitting close by him in the van and taking his arm as we walked through the cobbled streets. As a result, Eleni and I adopted one another. We sat together at meals, gathering morsels of lavash, string cheese, and hard-boiled eggs in white napkins from the sumptuous hotel buffets every morning and saving them for our long daytime journeys. After every stop, we looked out for each other and ensured that the other was on the bus at the appointed time. With her sparkling eyes, wry humor, and boundless energy, Eleni reminded me of my mother in her younger, healthier days, and I was grateful for her friendship.

Eleni's parents had both come from Chunkush, a two-hour drive from the Dudan Crevasse, and had managed to escape before the genocide. In Chunkush, as with the systematic extermination in other towns, first came a knock on the door of every Armenian household, then the demand that the men of the premises show themselves, and finally, the marching of the men to the Dudan Crevasse to die. Later, the women and children were rounded up and led to a similar fate.

Not far from the Crevasse, rock formations had created a set of ochre-colored caves. Eleni asked if we might all gather in one of the dank, musty interiors. The seventeen of us crowded into a small space. A match was lit, and Salpi, the actress, read some mournful lines written by Eleni's adult daughter in New York commemorating the genocide. We looked on solemnly.

Chills went up and down my spine. I wondered what the hell I was doing in this dirty, smelly cave in some far-off province of Turkey, listening to a poem by a woman I'd never met about a genocide I had thought so little about. Depression settled on me once again, and I gasped for air as I left the stifling cave.

We returned to the van, and Seljuk, our Turkish driver, drove us to the city center of Chunkush. We stopped at a small, white-washed home on a narrow street near the town center. A dark-skinned man in his 50s or 60s, heavily bearded and with several teeth missing, greeted us excitedly outside the small home, waving his arms frantically as our van approached. He welcomed us into the courtyard of his house. An ancient, shriveled woman, completely toothless, sat in the middle of the stark white square, grinning, her hair covered with a pale blue shawl.

The woman's name was Asiya. One hundred years before, in 1915, as Asiya's pretty Armenian mother waited to die on the edge of the Dudan Crevasse, a Turkish soldier had fancied her and taken the eleven-year-old girl as his wife, saving Asiya's mother from certain death. Asiya was born a few years later to the couple. As a result, this elderly, half-Armenian woman sitting before us, who had recently celebrated her 97th birthday, was the single person of any Armenian heritage still living in Chunkush, now a town made up mainly of Kurds. Sprawled out before her on the cement lay several American books and magazines gifted to her by another recent visitor, the Armenian American author Chris Bohjalian.

According to history, many young Armenian women, in last-ditch efforts to avoid death or deportation, married or were married off to Muslim men and forced to forfeit their families, their native Armenian tongue, their culture, and their Christian faith. Many refused to do so and died. Others, like Asiya's mother, converted to Islam and married to escape the fate of their mothers and fathers, sisters and brothers. Forbidden to speak of their pasts or true identities, most of these hidden Armenian children knew nothing of their Armenian parentage.

Elderly Asiya was one of the exceptions; encouraged by her Kurdish son-in-law, she welcomed Armenian pilgrims to a cup of tea in her courtyard, anxious to meet other Armenians like herself. She didn't speak much, and I don't remember the translation. I just watched her crooked smile and sad eyes, remnants of days long gone that would never again return for the Armenians of Chunkush.

What might I have done in Asiya's mother's position? Would I have renounced my faith, language, culture, and family to survive or refuse and suffer a horrible, certain fate? There is no easy answer, no "right" choice. Each choice carries nearly unbearable consequences, and I don't know what I might have done in her position.

But I am grateful for that warm day in July when Asiya welcomed us into her sun-bleached courtyard to share a fragment of our people's past with us.

Chapter 14

The Church at Diyarbakir

Heading southeast from Kharpert and Chunkush, we arrived in Diyarbakir. I had heard of Diyarbakir from Taline, my Armenian client, whose grandparents had been exiled from their home during the genocide. Other than that, I knew very little about the town, just another stop on this long journey east from Istanbul to the border of modern-day Armenia. We traversed the villages that make up what some Armenians call Western or Historic Armenia, refusing to acknowledge that these lands had belonged to Turkey for hundreds of years. Along the way, we also stopped in Zeitun for the Sarafian family from Long Island and Sanliurfa, Malatya, Elazig, and Van for the rest of the tour participants.

In Diyarbakir, we stopped at a large conglomeration of buildings and walked through a maze of cement walkways, passing preschools, offices, and cafés. Suddenly, a massive grey stone edifice loomed up before us. In front of the building, vendors sold souvenirs commemorating the 100th anniversary of the genocide, Armenian souvenirs bearing the distinctive Armenian script that I had come to recognize. These were the first souvenirs I'd encountered during our two-week trek East. Plates with ancient swirling Armenian designs in bright purples and blues and pins emblazoned with the number 100 in lush indigo to commemorate the anniversary were for sale on tables in front of the massive church.

As I entered the nave, I stopped short. Finally, a church that actually resembles a church, I thought, so unlike the dozens of crumbling stone ruins we'd encountered previously. Each of those ruins could only be identified by the tiny Armenian script etched into the ancient stone entrances or the emblematic carved crosses called "khachkars" embedded in the ochre stones, carvings so deep that no conversion by the Turks could erase them.

In every town we visited, Sarkis and Arpi would lead us to view these crosses, resembling a Celtic cross. At the time, I felt exasperated. We walked in the 100-degree heat to see this little cross etched into a stone. Or we'd drive hours to see a tiny line of Armenian script carved into the top of an ancient, crumbling building, now serving as a mosque, café, or Islamic community center. Only later, much later, years later, did I realize that they were showing us whatever they could of the remnants of our existence there. With little appreciation, I had walked around in a daze, not understanding Sarkis' lengthy explanations in Armenian and anxious to escape the enervating July heat.

But here, in the church at Diyarbakir, chairs were set up in front of a black wrought-iron gate protecting the main altar, awaiting parishioners. Five smaller altars adorned the sides of the church, replete with mosaics in blues, purples, and gold. Perched above the main altar stood a single gold cross in front of a painting of Mary and Jesus.

A series of grey arches led into the vast interior space considered the largest church in the Middle East. Along one side, small votives cast their dim light into the cavern. The beauty and solemnity struck me. One by one, Sarkis invited us to approach the center of the gate protecting the altar, motioning the rest of us to stay back and observe. I wasn't sure what I was supposed to do or why we were being invited to move forward individually. When it was my turn, I shyly approached the central altar of the church. I knelt as I had seen others do before me, assuming this must be an Armenian Catholic or Apostolic church rather than the Protestant church in which I was raised.

Suddenly, as I knelt there, tears streamed down my face. Embarrassed, I fought them back. I felt the presence of hundreds of Armenian souls flying around me, souls of those who may have worshiped here or who died during the extermination. The tears shocked me. Something about this church had struck a deep chord. I stayed there kneeling for a long time, although I'm sure it was really only a couple of minutes, unable to move and not wanting my tour mates to witness my tears. I rose, shaken, and lit a candle in the darkness at the back of the church to honor the Armenian ancestors lost in this town.

Outside, I bought a pin commemorating the 100th anniversary of the genocide and a small, colorful plate with jagged edges, not knowing what I would do with either. Now I use the little six-inch plate for my eggs in the morning or a sandwich at lunch, a gentle reminder of that day in Diyarbakir.

I learned later that this Church of St. Giragos in Diyarbakir was an Armenian Apostolic church designated as an Armenian place of worship in the 16th century. The Imperial German Army seized the church in 1913 and used it as their local headquarters during World War I. The church was closed during the genocide in 1915 and 1916, and in 1918, was converted into a fabric warehouse. The church wasn't returned to what was left of the small, local Armenian community until 1960, still in ruins.

In the 2000s, renovation began on the church, a sign of Turkish reconciliation with the Christian community as "Turkey's first church to be revived as a permanent place of worship." The refurbished church formally opened in 2012 for visitors and parishioners and was actively serving the small Armenian community that existed in Diyarbakir in 2015 when I visited.

In February 2016, less than a year after my visit, the church was heavily damaged during armed clashes between the Kurdistan Workers' Party and the Turkish Armed Forces. The Turkish government seized the church for its own uses, ending its short resurgence as an Armenian place of worship.

Learning this, my heart sank. Yet another remnant of our culture wiped out, I thought. I realized how privileged I had been to experience the church during the four short years when it had returned to its former glory as an Armenian place of worship.

Chapter 15

By the Banks of the Euphrates

*Take these seeds and plant them . . . they are the seeds of your becoming
. . . let these seeds become the great oak of who you are meant to become.*

~Alberto Villoldo, Ph.D.

I stood alone on a cliff edge on the banks of the Euphrates, staring at the still, blue-green river below me. Bare, brown rolling hills undulated in the glare of the summer sun. No boats on the river, no people on the shores, just that blue-green water against the tawny hills. All seemed serene as I gazed out at the horizon. I don't remember which town we were in that day, perhaps Elazig or Erzurum or somewhere en route from one to the other.

The midday July heat scorched, and I felt the dry, ochre earth crunch beneath my sandals. Then a slight breeze began to ripple the water twenty, maybe thirty feet below the rounded outcropping where I stood. The Sarafian family posed on the cliff next to me, laughing and giggling and wrapping their arms around one another, snapping cheerful selfies. My attention ricocheted between their raised voices and the still water beneath me.

Suddenly, in my mind's eye, as I gazed at the river, the blue disappeared, and I saw white waxen bodies float by, their limbs tangled together, one on top of the other, their streaming blood dying the azure
waters red. Their screams pierced the still afternoon. Dozens, maybe
hundreds of bodies, crowded up against the edge of the cliffs where
the Turkish gendarmes had bayoneted them and thrown them into the
river to die.

I wanted to scream and cry out with them, drop to my knees, and
tear off my clothing like some Old Testament widow, yell, scream, and
lash out at those Turkish soldiers in their crisp olive uniforms and
waxed mustaches.

"Stop!" I wanted to scream at those soldiers in my vision. "Stop!
Why are you killing my people?" But I said nothing. Instead, I got sick
to my stomach and quietly walked away, desperate to flee this inner
scene. Across the way, the Sarafians continued gleefully napping their
selfies.

My mind riveted back to a moment in Chile four years before. A
small group of us had crouched, hunched closely together at the bottom of a massive, conical-shaped volcano in central Chile. The volcano
sat like a sentry overlooking a large green lake.

We had come with friends to celebrate the date 11/11/2011,
deemed auspicious by our guides and teachers, Alberto Villoldo and
his wife, Marcela Lobos. At the time, I had no idea why they wished to
celebrate this date, but always eager to explore new places, Jim and I
had gladly agreed to accompany them on their tour of Chile. Much
later, I would learn that in numerology, the number 11 signifies the
grey area between two worlds, a tunnel leading from this world to another, and "the power to channel that which is invisible and unknown."

That morning in 2011, Alberto and Marcela had taken us on a ride
across the lake and down into the snow-laden volcano. A circular
wooden pathway wound its way around the inside of the volcano's
base, spiraling deep into the belly of the earth. We walked carefully on
the damp, slippery wooden slats, grasping the metal rails on either side
to steady us. The air smelled musty, and mist covered the wooden trail
and the muddy flanks of the volcano. Darkness surrounded us. We
inched our way down, one after another, until we reached the very
bottom of the volcano, where we huddled together in the small,
cramped space. Then, Alberto gave us seeds to scatter on the wet, dark

ground. He admonished us to toss them into the rich earth beneath us as a way of planting the seeds of whom we wished to become.

I thought then of my Armenian grandmother, who had appeared to me in the vision earlier that year at the Grand Canyon. I asked for her healing along with my own. I tossed the seeds into the red earth of Chile and vowed to plant new seeds on the soil of her homeland as a wish for the regeneration of her life and the 1.5 million Armenians who had died there almost 100 years before.

Now, here I was on the banks of the Euphrates in the homeland of my ancestors, thinking of Alberto's admonition. As I'd walked away from the cliff's edge, I remembered the packet of wildflower seeds I had brought from California tucked into the pocket of my purple linen skirt. I quickly returned to the river's edge, removed the packet from my pocket, and ripped it open.

I shook the seeds into the breeze. They ricocheted back at me, dropping around my feet, and scattering across the parched earth, cracked through the lack of moisture and vegetation, so unlike that rich red soil of Chile.

Doubting that anything could grow here on this crusty land, I threw the seeds nonetheless, as much to fulfill the promise I had made four years earlier at the bottom of that volcano in Chile than from any belief that they might bloom. I wondered if anything could ever regenerate here, whether the seeds of my American wildflowers or my ancient, traumatized Armenian culture.

I bowed my head in dejection and walked slowly back to the van, the gentle breeze billowing the folds of my skirt.

Chapter 16

Ani

O ur journey continued north and eastward toward the eastern border of Turkey and the present-day country of Armenia. We
parked outside the gates of the ancient, abandoned Armenian town of
Ani.

I stopped as I trudged through the fifteen-foot-high black wooden
gates that shielded the town from the street where Seljuk had left the
van. Stretched before me for what seemed like tens upon tens upon
tens of acres, sat crumbling, monolithic pink and ochre stone buildings
of every size and shape, dotting the dry, cracked, weed-strewn earth.
Each building stood alone as if in the center of its own sacred plot,
each in varying states of ruin and disrepair. No trees, no flowers, no
hint of green nor red or purple in the landscape, only the pink and
beige ochre of the decaying buildings. The area also seemed void of
living beings—no people, no birds, no life.

Some buildings resembled cathedrals, towering many stories high,
while others were smaller, more like chapels with their single, distinctive Armenian cupolas. Still others might have been homes or office
buildings, rectangular and lacking spires or pointed domes. But most
resembled skeletons of churches with halves of bell towers and naves
still intact, open to the dry air.

I stared at the bleak landscape, the buildings like the carcasses of
long-wrecked sailing vessels scattered throughout a sea of dust. I felt
an eerie sense of loneliness and trepidation. *What is this place?*

If Sarkis had described this ghost town of Ani to us in the van, once again, I either hadn't heard him, lost in my singular internal reverie, or hadn't understood his explanation in Armenian. Later, I learned that Ani was once the capital of the Bagratid Armenian kingdom between 961 and 1045, covering much of present-day Armenia and Eastern Turkey. Called the City of 1001 Churches, 50 churches, 33 cave churches, and 20 chapels had been excavated when I was there in 2015.

The town stood on a branch of the Silk Road and intersected with various trade routes between Turkey, Russia, Syria, and Iran. At their inception, many of Ani's religious buildings, palaces, and fortifications were among the world's most technically and artistically advanced structures. At its height, Ani was one of the world's largest cities, with a possible population of about 200,000.

I read that the Mongols sacked Ani in 1236 and that it never recovered from a devastating earthquake in 1319. It was gradually abandoned until, by the 17th century, it had been largely forgotten. Excavation of the ruins began in the early 20th century.

Ani has served as a cultural, religious, and national heritage symbol for Armenians, although I had never heard of it before my trip. It is one of the most visible and tangible symbols of past Armenian culture. In 2016, a year after I traveled to Western Armenia, Ani, like the Church at Diyarbakir and the cathedral of Hagia Sofia, was designated a World Heritage site.

After entering the gates, I took off to explore one of the churches at the western end of the vast plateau. Our group appeared to be alone in Ani on that hot July day. As a result, when a strange man followed me into a tiny chapel, I became concerned. Were single Western women safe in these parts of Turkey? Feeling the trepidation of being followed, I moved quickly away from the church's interior with its distinctive Armenian architectural dome.

I spied the rest of our group gathered together in the nave of a much larger cathedral nearby. I hurried quickly toward them. They stood in a large circle holding hands and singing an Armenian song I didn't recognize. They broke ranks and welcomed me into the circle. The music sounded dirge-like, and the faces of my colleagues were sober. Are they singing for our lost culture, paying homage to the hundreds of thousands of us who once lived here? My traveling companions all seemed to know the words and cadence of the song. I stood stiffly, feeling uncomfortable, like an imposter. I felt relieved when they stopped singing, and I could quickly take off again.

The present city of Ani sits high on a hill overlooking the Anhuryin River, which creates the border between Turkey and modern-day Armenia. As I walked toward the river, I saw Hayk, the nine-year-old elfin, always-smiling youngest child of the Sarafians. He ran ahead, beckoning me with outstretched arms to follow. A smile erupted in my heart at his energetic presence and desire for me to join him. I often felt excluded and on the periphery of this Armenian group, and I took delight in Hayk's invitation. We skipped toward another large church perched precariously on the hill overlooking the river, looking as if it could tumble headlong into destruction at any moment.

Hayk and I entered the church. As we looked up, we noticed partial remnants of pale pink, yellow, and blue frescoes of Jesus and his disciples staring down at us, fading against the ancient, crumbling walls. To my surprise, Hayk took my hand, and we sat silently for a moment, staring at those ancient symbols of our faith.

Something in this child, this crumbling church, this borderland between Armenia and Turkey touched me. I felt a sense of peace and belonging that I had failed to find earlier in the more immense cathedral.

As we left the church, I gazed at the rolling green hills and lush vegetation of modern-day Armenia, stark compared to Ani's cracked, dried ground behind me. I felt as if I could reach out and touch this present-day homeland of my people, yards away across the river. I knew, though, that the border was closed and impassable by land, as it has been since Armenia's 1992 skirmish with Azerbaijan.

Armenia, so close, yet so far away, I thought, not only physically, here, in this moment, but also, at times, metaphorically within my heart.

I thought about how Ani represented the remains of our Armenian culture here in Turkey, decimated, crumbling, and in ruins; the decaying churches were like skeletons of my people, void of sinew or substance, empty where they once were full.

Soon Hayk and I rejoined the group and returned to the van outside Ani's gates. Our last stop wasn't a place but a vista point on the side of a deserted highway. Green grass grew high on both sides of the street, and a gentle breeze greeted us as we got out of the van. In the distance, looming high above us, sat the perpetually snow-capped volcano of Mt. Ararat, its outline rising clearly from the vast flat plain.

Chapter 17

Mt. Ararat

L ike most Armenians, I have grown up with the name recognition and visual images of Mt. Ararat. My never-married Aunt Mary lived at the Ararat Home in Pasadena in her eighties, and my cousin Aline worked at another Ararat Home in the San Fernando Valley. Pictures of the great mountain appeared on posters and storefronts in the Armenian stores of Pasadena when I was growing up and on coasters at my aunt's house. The words "Mt. Ararat" have been a part of my family lexicon for as long as I can remember.

Legend has it that most of the time, grey clouds shroud Ararat's snow-covered peak; on this day, though, the white peak shimmered in the distance. Soon everyone in our group frantically posed for pictures in front of the legendary mountain before the clouds could move in. Arpi, one of our tour guides, and my eighty-seven-year-old friend Eleni threw their arms around me and encouraged me to smile as cameras started clicking.

I didn't know what to think or feel, with everything happening so quickly. I stepped away from the clicking cameras and gazed at the mountain, trying to feel its presence. Mt. Ararat, I thought. I can't believe I'm actually here.

The mountain has been called Ararat in the West since the Middle Ages and came to be identified with the mountains of Ararat described in the Bible as the resting place of Noah's Ark. Despite lying within present-day Turkey and outside the borders of modern Armenia, Mt. Ararat serves as the principal national symbol of Armenia. It is considered sacred by most Armenians and features prominently in Armenian literature and art. It is depicted on the coat of arms of Armenia along with Noah's Ark. Many historians and Biblical scholars agree that Ararat is the Hebrew name of Urartu, the geographical predecessor of Armenia.

In the aftermath of the genocide, the mountain came to represent the destruction of the native Armenian population of Eastern Turkey. It symbolized Armenian efforts to reclaim the "lost lands" which are now part of Turkey and which held a significant Armenian population before the genocide.

Lying geographically in Turkey but representing Armenia and Armenians, Mt. Ararat bridges these two estranged and often warring nations. This volcano burrows deep into the hot molten earth and stretches high into the heavens. Noah's mythical ark, built in the almond shape of the mandorla, landed here, joining the masculine and feminine of each species, bringing together opposites to form a central whole. The joining place of disparate aspects—the Armenian and Turkish, heaven and earth, masculine and feminine—Ararat stood in the middle of the mandorla, integrating something within my heart.

I felt deep, inner peace while gazing at the snow-glazed peak. My ancestors before me had stood in this place, gazing at this sight for centuries. From the womb of this volcano, on this vast Anatolian plain, according to legend, my culture was birthed. I experienced a sense of awe at finally finding recognition of my ancestral home here in Turkey after witnessing the desolation of Ani and the horrors of the previous two weeks of the Genocide Tour.

I reflected on the tour and the moments that brought me here. The moments of revulsion and the moments of deep resonance that had touched me: the visions of bloodied bodies floating down the Euphrates, the frescoes of the cathedral in Ani, and the tears of recognition in Kharpert and the Church at Diyarbakir. I thought back on meeting Asiya in Chunkush and drinking tea on her cement patio as she displayed books by Chris Bohjalian. Her Armenian mother had survived the massacre of the Dudan Crevasse, unlike the ten thousand other Armenian bodies left there to die.

The horrific with the sacred, the tragic with the beautiful. They had all joined together to bring me to this moment, an Armenian-American woman standing in front of this symbol of her people, as familiar to her as the stars and stripes of the United States.

Here I felt the Armenian within my soul in ways I had not felt before, peering at random crosses etched into rocks on the side of the road or witnessing cursive scratchings of the Armenian language I could not decipher on the walls of abandoned Armenian houses.

This may be what I came here looking for, after all, I thought.

Here in front of Mt. Ararat, there were no visions of long strings of women marching into the desert or executions in town squares. Here I felt hope for a people that had survived and continues to survive against near-unbelievable odds, a group as ancient as the snow-covered peak. My heart filled, and I felt, if for one brief moment, at home in this motherland that had often felt so alienating. I gazed at Hayk joking and laughing nearby, on the side of the road with 87-year-old Eleni, the young joining with the old, the American with the Armenian, and me standing somewhere between them.

I returned to the van with a full heart and gratitude for this journey.

Chapter 18

The Aftermath

Later that summer, after I returned home from the Genocide Tour, I tossed and turned every night, trying to relax my tense limbs. I'd wake up gasping for breath and trying to still the fear beating in my heart. My legs trembled, and I had to throw my walking shoes on every morning and pace the surrounding hills to survive my long hours sitting at the office. I felt unhinged.

During those nocturnal awakenings, whitish-gray, ghoulish, disembodied souls surrounded me, frantically reaching out and stretching their diaphanous white arms toward me. There were hundreds of them in all shapes and sizes.

They frightened me. I felt their fear, as well as my own.

An image appeared that I had first seen in meditation before beginning the Genocide Tour; a giant wooden ladder standing on four legs, stretching far into the heavens beyond where I could see. One by one, and sometimes in groups, some unseen force led me to guide the swirling souls to the ladder to help them make their journey to the light on the other side. Sometimes I climbed the ladder with them. Other times I just pointed the way. I exhorted the reluctant souls to trust me, to go toward the light, and to leave the harsh locations of their tragic deaths behind.

I don't know how I knew to help these beings on their journeys to the other side. I just did. Each night, sleep came only after I had ferried all of that night's souls up the ladder.

Am I going crazy? I wondered. What the heck is going on here? I didn't volunteer for this. At least, I am not aware of having volunteered for this. I want it to stop. I don't want to do this.

During the first few weeks, the souls came in droves, crowding around the ladder until I showed them how to climb its rungs. As the summer wore down, fewer and fewer souls appeared. Did I get them all? Have they all gone now? Then suddenly, I was transported to Dachau, to Auschwitz, ferrying more souls, this time from the Holocaust rather than the Armenian Genocide, or so I imagined.

Am I making this up? I wondered. I knew I wasn't dreaming. I knew I was awake because I couldn't sleep until all of that night's souls had disappeared. I better call a psychiatrist, I thought. Something is definitely wrong with me.

Then one day, they were gone. I slept through the nights, and no one disturbed me. The ladder stood alone on a barren field, if it appeared at all. Souls no longer crowded its base. However, the fear and the anxiety remained with me for a long while.

A year later, Sarkis let us know that Seva Sarafian and her daughter Pari were coming to town to attend a conference put on by the UCLA Armenian Studies department. "What a great opportunity to get together for a reunion with the Southern California contingent of our group," he said. Sarkis arranged the dinner at the home of the older couple, Narin and Aram, from South Pasadena.

After arriving at Narin and Aram's place, I sat stiffly, my hands clasped in my lap, around the square dinner table covered in white plastic, waiting for the guests of honor. Sitting at that table in downtown South Pasadena, munching on the carrots, celery, and hummus set out for hors-d'oeuvres, thousands of miles from the Genocide Tour, I felt nervous. Finally, around 9:45, Seva and Pari bounded in, full of smiles and hugs for everyone, having thoroughly enjoyed the Armenian conference across town.

Seva and Pari sat down as Narin hurriedly placed the pilaf, manti, and kufte on the table for all of us to share. I looked hesitantly around the table at Sarkis and the others: Salpi; the attractive young actress; the elderly couple Aram and Narin; and our other tour guide, Arpi. There was a subject I'd wanted to broach.

I looked at Sarkis, a half glance, unable to meet his eyes. "I got depressed after our trip last year. Did anyone else get depressed?" I asked tentatively, looking around the table.

Seven pairs of dark eyes stared blankly back at me. Had they not gotten depressed, or were they just not wanting to admit it?

"I mean, going to all those genocide sites and talking about it. It got to me."

Sarkis looked up from his plateful of manti, peering at me over the thick black glasses resting on his 73-year-old nose. "You were unprepared," he said quickly, looking down, forking another piece of the stuffed square manti pasta into his mouth.

"What do you mean?" I asked, my heart quivering.

"Your family didn't prepare you. We all grew up talking about the Genocide. You didn't."

How did Sarkis know what my family talked about? But I also knew he was right.

While Sarkis had met my parents and my sister, I had no sense that he knew them well. He was a friend of my Aunty Gladys, but our family had never attended his church, and I had certainly never interacted with him before this tour.

Seva chimed in, eyes dancing and smiling widely at the group, "Yes, my parents and grandparents always told us how their little town of Zeitoun held off the Turks for ten days before surrendering. It gave me such pride in my family and we Armenians."

"I grew up in Aleppo, close to the genocide, with my refugee parents. There was no escaping it. We lived with it daily," continued Sarkis, his voice a monotone.

Now it was my turn to stare blankly. The knot in my stomach grew larger and heavier.

"Why do you think my family didn't talk about it?" I asked quietly, unable to touch the food I'd waited so long to eat. I desperately wanted to have some understanding and justification for my family's silence.

"They were different. They wanted to fit in and acculturate. They wanted to forget," Sarkis continued, almost offhandedly, still focused on his food.

I didn't know how to respond. For the rest of the evening, I again sat quietly, my hands clenched in my lap, my stomach churning, feeling as I had often felt on the tour, that I was somehow deficient as an Armenian. I didn't speak the language, I didn't attend an Armenian church, and I knew so little about the history of my people. I teetered back and forth between the American and the Armenian within me, mostly feeling very American and, less frequently, Armenian.

But later, I remembered staring up at the peak of Mt. Ararat, feeling the fullness of my ancient heritage and resting in that almond-shaped center of the mandorla, both a proud Armenian and proud American at the same time.

I wanted to return to that feeling, over and over again, if only to continually remind myself of who I was.

SECTION THREE

Thoughts on Culture and Identity During a Global Pandemic

In March 2020, the international pandemic touched every one of us and isolated most of us within our homes. Unable to travel outwardly, I traveled inwardly through writing in my journals and drafting this memoir.

Locked in the liminal space between inner and outer worlds, I pondered the nature of transgenerational trauma, the power of my ancestor's Christian faith, the possible etiology of my lifeline struggle with depression, and the very heart of home and existence.

During that time, a war in distant Armenia escalated, causing repercussions in the Southern California Armenian community and within my soul. This section contains journal entries written in the first terrifying months of the pandemic, slightly edited to provide context for the reader.

Chapter 19

March 2020

. . . and there shall be a plague upon the land . . .

It's been fourteen days, and Alicia still refuses to come home, terrified that she will infect us with the virus she's had for the past two weeks. She'd returned to LA from her final weekend of her Master's degree with a fever, a sore throat, and a cough. Stress, we thought, no big deal. It was an emotional weekend, the end of a program she had loved and the leave-taking of a group of people she had grown attached to. We hadn't been at all concerned.

But Alicia felt differently. Her symptoms mimicked precisely those of the coronavirus spreading throughout the globe: fever, fatigue, sore throat, and a lingering dry cough. She'd holed herself up in her pea-sized Los Angeles apartment alone for the past two weeks, though her fever had dissipated days before. I suggested that she probably was no longer contagious and was safe to come home. But Alicia, a letter-of-the-law kind of gal, refused to see us until every trace of her symptoms had disappeared. With no virus test kits in sight, she played it safe, terrified that something might happen to her parents if she came anywhere near us.

When Alicia sets her mind to something, there's no dissuading her. She read *Eating Animals* and *Forks over Knives* when she was 14, and no bite of flesh, chicken broth, refried beans, or pie crusts made with lard have knowingly passed her lips since. I should know better than to try to change Alicia's mind about anything.

———————————

Today she left her tiny apartment for the first time, gathering the courage to drop by in her little white VW to pick up some food we'd ordered for her. We dropped the three white canvas Trader Joe's bags just inside the front gate, which divides our driveway from the street. She picked up the bags and blew us a hug and a kiss. I cried, not believing that even after fourteen days, she wouldn't come into the house and say hello. She refused even to pet Ralph, her beloved little black dog, fearing she might somehow contaminate him. A dog. I seethed inwardly beneath my tears, quietly cursing her tendency toward anxiety and over-caution. I was worried about the effects upon her of too many days and weeks of isolation.

I have often worried about this anxiety that Alicia has struggled with for over a decade. Where did it come from? What might we have done to engender it? Neither Jim nor I have struggled much with anxiety. Well, I struggled with it after the Genocide Tour and now during the pandemic, but not as a child or young adult. Depression, yes, but anxiety, not so much. We tried to provide as stable an environment as possible for her growing up.

I wondered, is everyone anxious these days, or is it something else that has lived within her these many years? Does her soul also carry imprints from the DNA passed down from the traumas suffered decades ago by my grandparents and their parents before them? Did the anxiety skip a generation and blossom within Alicia?

———————————

Very quickly, there are no more decisions to be made. Gone are the days of shall I go to work or not? Is it safe to go out to eat? Can I walk around the Rose Bowl with the two friends I've walked with every Monday morning for almost twenty years? Everything has closed down and become forbidden, particularly for those over 60: restaurants, movie theatres, retail stores, libraries, and even beaches, parks, and hiking trails. All of California is on lockdown, with only trips to the grocery store, Target, the doctor's office, and the pharmacy allowed. My trip to Ireland for the "Awakening the Genie Within" seminar, the Thomas Merton/Mary Oliver conference, my memoir class retreat, the holotropic breath work seminar with Stan Grof at Esalen, my women's group, and my book club, all canceled.

We hunker down at home, walking endless times around the block to quell anxiety and get some exercise, careful to remain at least six feet from the kids riding bikes and the dog walkers. We run into neighbors we haven't seen in years now that everyone is required to shelter in place. A local ob-gyn, a close friend of my brother, is on a ventilator with the virus in the Pasadena hospital where I was born.

The virus creeps closer.

Rain, unusual for this time of year in Los Angeles, darkens the already dark days, the external mirroring the internal. It heightens the ominous feeling of the dystopia we've entered. Every morning I awaken not *from* a nightmare but *into* one. The birds harmonizing outside my bedroom window awaken me gently, with a smile on my heart, only to fade into a frown when I remember that the world has now changed, perhaps irrevocably, as this killer virus spreads like fluid, invisible mucus upon the Earth.

Fear runs in and out of our consciousness, arriving at unforeseen times. Fear of the terror outside our doors that might break in and enter at any time. Fear of loss, death, and what we can't control.

Though this pandemic differs from a genocide, might this be some of what my ancestors felt long ago in Turkey when the terror outside *their* doors threatened to enter and transform their worlds forever? I am not accustomed to living with this kind of fear. I wonder if my grandparents, as second-class minorities in a Turkish culture that reviled them, became accustomed to this fear.

Does anyone become accustomed to this kind of fear?

I've been wearing my sweats for days. The daily ritual of showering, hair, makeup, and dressing before driving to work has halted. It feels freeing yet weird. Finally, I change into my favorite pair of tight black jeans. Already they stretch tight against my belly, cutting into my flesh. The legs chafe and bunch up against my groin. And it's only been two weeks.

All I want to do is eat. I want crunchy. I want sweet. I want salty potato chips. French bread slathered with avocado, spoonfuls of the

Jiffy peanut butter I buy for our dog Ralph, and white rice dripping with fresh parmesan. I crave comfort foods I have not indulged in for years. My fruit and veggies dwindle. Is it safe to go out to the grocery store to replenish them? We stay home as much as possible, ordering our food online from Ralphs. All our other local food stores no longer accept orders for deliveries, overwhelmed at the moment by the demand of an entire nation on lockdown.

Initially, I make bottomless bowls of homemade chicken soup and fruit salad. I cut up garlic and gulp it with water, trying to stay healthy. One of Jim's clients from New York City, guilt-ridden after ordering too many zinc lozenges when they were still available, sent us zinc gummies, zinc lozenges, and zinc capsules. I gulp them along with my garlic.

Then one morning, I let Jim go to the "seniors only" hour from 7-8 a.m. at our local Vons. I text him a carefully curated list of things we need: three large tomatoes, a head of romaine, some Vitamin D, a red and green bell pepper, eggs, brown rice, seedless green grapes, and almond milk.

I should know about Jim's tendency toward excess by now. Upon his return, I first notice the sixteen huge, red, green, and yellow peppers packaged in cardboard containers and the smaller bag of mixed mini peppers wrapped in cellophane. "What are we going to do with all these peppers?" I ask him in desperation.

"You said you wanted peppers," he replies. "They'll keep."

Then I see the four quarts of strawberries. My eyes get big.

"What's up with the strawberries, Jim?"

"They were on sale. I thought you liked strawberries."

I already have an unfinished pint in the fridge that has been there for two weeks. Jim doesn't eat strawberries, and Alicia won't come around.

Then out come the two huge bags of potatoes, in addition to the one I already have in the drawer, eight giant tomatoes, two jumbo bags of jalapeño Kettle chips, four bags of cheddar cheese fishies, a giant loaf of French bread and three jumbo bags of Cheetos. For two people.

"We need comfort food at a time like this," he says. I find out later that he hid a final bag of Fritos and chocolate chips in his car.

I haven't seen a bag of Cheetos or cheddar fishies since Alicia was in grammar school. Now I have three of one and four of the other. You'd think Jim was the descendant of starving Armenians, not me, I think. I groan loudly, watching the 17 pounds I managed painstakingly to lose last year packing themselves back on.

I don't confess to him that I ordered two pre-made graham cracker pie crusts from the market last week, ready to be filled with the lemons and apples that weigh down our backyard trees: Dutch Apple Pie, Lemon Meringue Pie. I fantasize about which I might make first. I haven't made a pie in over a year, but this isolation thing is bringing out the worst in both of us regarding food.

I stretch out on my living room couch, perusing recipes for strawberry pie. I've never made a strawberry pie before. Lemon meringue, apple? Sure. But never strawberry. What else can I possibly do with four quarts of strawberries?

Now that I work at home, I have set up a makeshift office in Alicia's room, stacking files for each day's clients in neat piles. I've brought home letterhead stationary, envelopes, stamps, and work supplies from my office in Pasadena. I try to adjust to working with Zoom for those clients who need to see my face accompanying my voice. I growl at having to wash my face, brush my hair, and put on makeup for the camera. I growl, but I do it. With the rain, Jim and I trade off working remotely with our clients in front of the fire in the living room. When the sun shows her face, which is rare nowadays, we work from the front and back porches.

Last night, after a particularly rough session with a young woman whose heroin-addicted boyfriend had relapsed, I lay on the sofa listening to the soundtrack from *Rent*, my favorite musical, trying to calm my frazzled nerves. *Rent* sings the saga of a group of young people living in New York City in the 1980s, struggling with the effects of a different virus that overtook the land: AIDS. Tears come to my eyes as I remember when that virus spread throughout the world, taking friends and colleagues with it.

And here we are again—another plague upon the land.

Advertisements for clothing crop up on my computer screen as I peruse the latest bad news. Clothing, I think. I no longer need clothing, living as I am in my jammies, jeans, and sweatshirts. I eye the black pants and silk blouses, and flouncy skirts in red, orange, and taupe, with their array of fitted jackets lying untouched in my closet. They seem so irrelevant now, colored bits of cloth hanging on their skeletons of air.

In times of trauma, the emphasis on mundane things that once seemed important diminishes. Life takes on a different perspective. It's no wonder Grandmother Jemela may not have been as concerned about the excess weight on her sturdy frame as I have been. Forced out of her country of origin, married to a man she hardly knew, and unable to work outside the home, she likely had more significant concerns than appearances to worry about.

I see the dress I'd set aside for the once-in-a-lifetime family reunion planned for this Easter Sunday. Armenian relatives from Dad's family whom we hadn't seen in decades had arranged to fly in from all over the country. Ancestral pictures had been gathered and made into a video; family trees had been circulated and filled in, name tags prepared, and a vast Armenian feast planned. I'd sent pictures from our wedding and photos of Alicia since she was two.

Now the dress will remain unworn, the pictures unseen, and the family trees set to gather dust until the reunion can occur at some unforeseen future time. Families separated into their tight little worlds, not knowing when, if ever, they will meet again.

Despite his ridiculous buying habits, I am grateful for Jim, for someone to discuss every passing fear and worry with, someone to keep me looking at the big picture. Someone to walk with, drive with, and cook with. I count myself among the lucky, as I have so often in my life, to have him, at least when we're not sniping at each other over some triviality. I worry about my clients and friends, particularly the single, extroverted ones who could hardly stand to be alone for even one day, let alone 14 or 28, or 64.

And now it is Tuesday morning when I usually walk up and down the hills of my little town with my friend Deanna. The sun bobs in and out from behind the clouds, and the rain has momentarily fled. Questions fill my mind. Do I or don't I? Is it safe if we stay six feet apart? Will we stay six feet apart? With my deaf ear, will I even be able to hear Deanna if we walk six feet apart? The agonizing decision-making begins anew. Should I or shouldn't I? I know what Alicia would say, but I'm sure not going to ask her. "No. No. No." That is her answer to anything and everything I want to do. Alicia has exhorted me to be careful with how much I see my friends, even outdoors, on walks. "Please, please be careful," she says in her strained, anxious voice. I hear the child's terror that something will happen to her mother, no matter how old the child is. I remember the same feeling when my parents were alive. I am relieved that they are no longer here and that I don't have to worry about them during this time of isolation.

Should I take the chance and enjoy a walk with a close friend or play it safe? I am not made for these kinds of decisions. So I go.

At night as I fall asleep, I feel a tug on my heart from the direction of China, where the virus started. I push it away. Yesterday, in my meditation, the tug came from over Italy. I don't say anything to anyone about these tugs. They are familiar to me from the days after the Genocide Tour when I was asked to ferry deceased souls to the other side.

One day, out of the blue, Jim asks if I've been contacted to shepherd souls deceased from the coronavirus to the other side.

I narrow my eyes and glare at him. "What makes you ask?"

"Just wondering," he responds.

"Yes," I answer quietly.

"Have you done it?"

"No, I'm not ready."

I remember all too well those tense days after the tour when disembodied souls haunted my nights. Forces I neither knew nor understood beckoned me to help, lest I lose precious sleep and sanity. I am not anxious to experience those mysterious, nocturnal journeys again.

But the next night, in meditation, I find myself above Milan amidst a vast congregation of souls. Once again, as I did after the Genocide Tour, I walk with those souls willing to go up that tall wooden ladder to the lands beneath the stars. I talk gingerly with the reluctant, suggesting they move toward the light and may be more helpful to their loved ones on the other side. I haven't had the heart to hover over China, Iran, Madrid, Paris, or New York. But Italy is a country close to my heart, a place where I studied art history as an undergraduate and a place that I love. At this point, it is also the country hardest hit by the virus.

Amidst the myriad of videos, poems, and spiritual treatises flying around on the Internet, I take comfort in a short quote by the monk Thomas Merton: "You do not need to know precisely what is happening or exactly where it is all going. What you need is to recognize the possibilities and challenges offered by the present moment and to embrace them with courage, faith, and hope."

So I meditate more; with more time, I read the spiritual missives in my inbox from Eckhart Tolle, Pema Chödrön, Richard Rohr, David Steindl-Rast, and Matthew Fox, each with their assessment of our current situation. I spend more time soaking in the morning light shining through my bedroom window, watching how the rays splinter through the pines. I really see the green and red feathers of the hummingbirds hovering over our front-porch feeders as they drink the sugared nectar, flapping their delicate wings. All the birds know it is spring and have come in greater numbers than ever this year to serenade us. No longer rushing to get up, shower, and work, I listen intently to their song.

The South American shamans, the Indian gurus, and even some Christian theologians suggest that this virus has come to give Mother Gaia a chance to heal. For the air to clear from too much pollution, the waters to cleanse from toxicity, and the animals to be allowed to flourish freely. Perhaps it is also a time for us to heal from the frenzied pace of everyday life, the rampant seduction of materialism, and the unbounded greed and narcissism of our world leaders. Perhaps these are some of the possibilities and opportunities of which Merton speaks.

Who knows what the world will look like post-virus? What will we create, born of this moment in our world's history? What, if anything, have we learned from other pandemics? What, if anything, have we learned from war and genocide? Can we, will we, do it differently next time?

Chapter 20

April 2020

A s experts warn us to brace ourselves for these next two weeks of April, we begin the fourth week of sheltering-in-place. They predict the most significant number of deaths here in California and in the U.S. since this madness started. Today, the state of New York reached an all-time high for its daily death toll: 779. We are encouraged not to go out now, even to grocery stores and pharmacies.

Life begins to take on a new rhythm of regularity with the virus, though certain rituals from our previous life remain. Jim continues to get up at 6:30 every morning, awakened by Ralph scratching at his bedcovers to let him know that it's time to get moving. Jim gives Ralph his morning massage, stretching our dog across his chest. Ralph whines with delight as Jim rubs his neck, chest, and tummy.

They hop out of bed. Jim drags on his now fraying, filthy Stanford Sierra Camp sweatshirt and the Levis he dropped on the floor the night before. He pads to the kitchen, grabs the leash, and out they go for their morning sojourn. Today, unlike other days, Jim wears one of the blue cloth masks that the local Chinese Mother's Club has donated to all the seniors in the neighborhood. The mayor of Los Angeles, Eric Garcetti, now mandates that we wear masks whenever we leave the house.

Upon Jim's return, he reports on which of his regular walking pals he has not encountered. Bodhi and Fluff, the "dogs with the two mothers," as Jim calls them, haven't been seen in weeks, and today strange cars are parked outside their home. Jim worries that they are sick and quarantined in their house.

No sight either of the elderly Korean couple, always decked in heavy colorful sweatshirts zipped up to their necks, rain or shine. The man always walks a few steps in front of his wife, his pace faster; sometimes, he even laps her. The couple speaks little English. For decades, we have communicated through smiles and waves as we've passed each other, circumambulating the block. We wonder, where are they? What's happening behind all the shut doors and pulled curtains?

Worry and uncertainty creep into our days. I think of those days in Turkey over a hundred years ago. Did they worry about who would be next, when the knock on the door would usher their father or grandfather out to the town square? Or when they would be marched away from their homes, never to return? I cannot compare my present situation with theirs, but sometimes this fear triggers that deeper, far more terrifying one.

Jim woke up in the middle of the night last night, called by unseen forces to begin performing the death rites on the forty-five-year-old English teacher who lives around the corner. He teaches at a local high school that Alicia attended as an adolescent. With his right hand, Jim gradually unwound all the teacher's chakras from his physical body and sealed them, letting his energy body float up past his physical body. Michael, the teacher, has been in the ICU on a respirator with the virus for nearly three weeks.

I, too, woke up this morning sensing a difference in Michael, a movement away from, rather than toward, his terrified family. I am frightened and desperately hope that we are wrong in our tracking of this situation.

The doctors are telling Michael's wife, Claire, and their two college-aged children, hunkered down in the Tudor house on the cul-de-sac around the corner, to prepare for the worst. That he may not make it. Though I have only met Michael once and do not know him well, I empathize with his family. I know too well the feeling of sitting vigil for a family member who hovers on the razor-thin precipice between life and death. I pray, send healing light over the family and Michael, and cleanse his chakras whenever possible. I even beg for his survival, as I did when my brother sat on this razor's edge, unconscious in a

German ICU ten months ago. But my brother's wife and kids constantly rotated around his bed, talking with him, begging him to return to them, telling him funny stories, and praying over him.

No such luck for Michael. His wife Claire has the virus herself, isolated in her home while her two kids care for her. No one is allowed by Michael's bedside, of course, as no one is permitted by the bedsides of the thousands of individuals tethered to ventilators throughout the world.

I'm gratified to hear that Michael and his family are people of faith. I pray that their faith brings them solace at this time. I think about the sustaining Christian faith of my parents and my grandparents, a faith passed down from generation to generation among Armenians since the 4th century. I remember how often my parents and aunt attributed any good fortune in their lives to the grace of God rather than any effort of their own.

There was a plaque above the door of my father's study, painted in fading hues of red, green, and blue: "God Heals. The Doctor Takes the Fee." As a child, I pondered the meaning of that plaque. I took it to heart as an adult when I opened my own office. I hope faith also somehow sustained my grandparents as they dealt with the terror of the killings outside their doors and the uncertainty of starting a life in the New World.

All communication now takes place through technology: FaceTime, Skype, Zoom, and WhatsApp. Venmo provides me with instantaneous deposits of money, so different and more convenient than the checks and cash I have received from clients for thirty-five years.

This period feels like the science fiction movies of my youth when futuristic aliens with pointy heads and long, smooth, plastic-covered limbs communicated through robotic machines or telepathically, never touching. That, or a high-tech return to farm life before the Industrial Revolution when everyone worked at home, ate at home, and spent evenings with their families. We seem now to have entered the world of the future and the past simultaneously. I and many others have difficulty believing this surreal existence exists.

I imagine my ancestors may have felt the same, incredulous and unbelieving, when driven from their ancient lands through no fault of their own.

Half an inch of gray roots now grows along my hairline. I imagine how many more inches will grow before this craziness subsides. My friend Kim now sports a three-quarter-inch streak of gray hair on either side of the part, dividing her long. straight auburn hair. My hairstylist puts together color kits to send to her clients and YouTube videos explaining how to apply them.

Ingenuity crops up in all shapes, sizes, and colors during this unprecedented time.

I doubt I will go so far as to order a color kit. It might be interesting to see how I will look as a "grey head." Vanity at a time like this seems superfluous.

But not for everyone. An MD friend of mine who runs a Med Spa which I've ascertained is code for a place where people purchase cosmetic procedures, sneaks into her office several times a week to freshen up the Botox injections and face lifts that her celebrity clientele feel they cannot live without. With time on their hands now, her clients are eager to freeze off that extra layer of fat on their waists and underarms and to get the beauty procedures they can't usually fit into their hectic schedules—some of the services deemed "essential" in Los Angeles during the coronavirus.

I worry for my friend working in her office during this mandatory "shelter-in-place." She worries about how to pay her employees and her mortgage if she doesn't, like so many others worldwide.

My heart catches in my throat as the anchors on MSNBC and CNN report the death tolls mounting daily. Spain and Italy have been hit particularly hard. I think back again to the time I studied art history as an undergraduate in Florence and taught English as a second language in Spain the year after college.

Though I had no experience teaching and spoke little Spanish, save what I remembered from high school, I gamely showed up to class five days a week and winged it through the day's lessons. I loved every moment: the people streaming the streets at all hours of the day, sipping cafe con leche and eating tortas along the avenues, or tossing back a vino tinto at dusk in the bars. The hospitality of the people and my students, always willing to take me for a copa de vino or a churro con chocolate after class, warmed my heart.

In Spain, my soul resonated deeply with something missing from the new-world shininess of my Southern California upbringing. I loved the monumental ancient churches dotting the street corners and the warmth of the Spaniards kissing me on both cheeks every time we met. I felt the deep faith of the traditional Catholic culture and the emphasis on relationships rather than acquisition and appearances. I felt the depth and resonance of an ancient culture not so different from the one my ancestors left behind.

In this fourth week, I acclimate better to our physical-distancing life, setting up the routines of meditating, showering, working, walking, reading, cooking, and eating. As before, Jim and I fight over the temperature gauge in the house: he turns the heat off, and I turn the heat on. He turns it off. I turn it on. He opens all the doors; I close them. He opens all the doors. I close them. We repeat this ritual throughout the days, as we have for years.

I find avocado pits hidden throughout the house, under the cedar chest in the bedroom, splayed on the oriental rug in the dining room, and under the pink, quilted coverlet on our king-sized bed. It's avocado season here in Southern California, and our dog loves to devour those avocados that the birds and squirrels drop from our four trees.

In these ways, life marches on in our little suburb. I admit to sometimes enjoying the peace and not feeling obligated to attend the many Armenian family gatherings, book clubs, women's groups, and random social engagements that normally litter my calendar.

But as I peruse my journals, I am reminded that this has not always been the case.

I am not doing well. I am not rising to the occasion and am not proud of it. I am not the paragon of calm and loving spirituality I wish to be. I am an angry ball of venom. And it's not pretty. It's best to stay out of my way.

Sometimes, I am angry at everyone: my daughter, my husband, and my friends. Rage spills out of me, anger that has been there for millennia, rage at powerlessness, and trapped-ness and no way out but in. I don't want to go inward right now. I want to get out. I want to walk on the beach and go away alone on a solitary pilgrimage to who knows where. I want out, and there is No Exit. No way out but in. And I'm pissed about it.

I am a fire-breathing dragon spewing out great black, pulsing, molten lava orbs of rage. I have become a conduit of rage, not only for the rage of the world but for the inner, unexpressed, unexplored anger of my ancestors.

Some nights, I awaken between 3 and 4 a.m. having trouble catching my breath and gently gasping for air. Off and on for an hour, I take slow deep breaths, in eight counts through the nose, out eight counts through the mouth. Every time I stop the breathing, the shortness of breath returns. I begin again until I can go back to sleep for a couple more hours. I know this is not the shortness of breath said to be a symptom of the virus. I know this particular shortness of breath. It comes daily, an acquaintance who hasn't visited in quite a long time. Now she visits daily. At least I know what to do when she arrives.

Sometimes, though, I feel like it is happening again and that I am becoming unhinged, like after the Genocide Tour, traversing back and forth between crazy and present reality.

Then, one night, the anger and anxiety suddenly open within me and disappear, as if providing a portal to another world. I find myself above Spain, shepherding souls killed by the virus, gently letting the confused know they have died, ferrying the willing ones up toward the light, and returning to comfort the hesitant.

After the rage, peace and a sense of bliss descend upon me. Here I do not feel anger, only calm and a sense of gratitude. Some souls are sad, some angry, and most are disoriented, unaware of what has happened to them. But what I feel is liberation. They have been liberated from their bodies. Maybe they are the lucky ones, I think. I feel horrible and heretical for saying this, but in the ethers above Spain, I strongly feel the peace and liberation from sick and ailing bodies. I am happy for them, as I was when my father died eighteen years before, jubilant at his final release from the body paralyzed and mute for the previous thirteen years.

I know this is not a popular notion. It's not one I have reasoned out. It's just descended upon me. As I return to my body, I feel the familiar fear and rage at the world situation, a rage with no object, just cursing out into the atmosphere. But there, shepherding the souls, I felt bliss, freedom, and love.

I wonder, how much of this rage is transgenerational? How has this pandemic tapped into some deeper well of dislocation and anger at events beyond my control?

Panic, peace, fear, anger, gratitude: they all bump up against each other, with their different sensations, intensities, and bodily reactions in this soup of emotions that boils within me. I try to remain calm, to remind myself that this too shall pass, but it isn't easy. It's difficult to know that people are dying, not just all over the world, but outside my door. I am grateful for my safety, but grief-stricken at the experience of others who are not so safe.

Carrying around all these emotions has been hard for me in this life. Sometimes I would welcome a liberation of my own, but I know I am not yet ready to leave.

Later, I realize I can travel wherever I want in the universe in my imagination if I allow myself to. First, I am in our mountain house in Lake Arrowhead, then in the gentle brown hills of Corfu, the highlands of the Himalayas, and the peaks of the Andes, free to travel among the stars and into other worlds. My consciousness soars free, and I no longer feel chained to these four walls.

My friend Karen's memoir describes her near-death experience at age ten. In that experience, while dead, she felt peace and bliss, realizing that this life, this world in which we live, is but a dream, and we are only actors within it. In these dark times, I take comfort in the thought that we might awaken from this nightmare into some different, less anxiety-provoking, more peace-filled world.

A young college-student client, now stuck at home with her parents, says she feels a strange sense of peace, unified with everyone else in this shared experience. "We all fear the same fear, are living the same reality," she tells me. "I take comfort in that."

Another client, a usually kind and soft-spoken orthopedic nurse working at a local hospital, swears vehemently and sobs in our phone session for the first time in the five years I have known her. "Fuck them all. Goddamnit! Why are they doing this to us?" Like all nurses in her hospital, she has been asked to rotate through the coronavirus wards, treating the sick and dying virus patients. "I'm not prepared for this. I did not sign up for this," she rages. "If I could, I would quit, but I can't. I didn't volunteer to put my life at risk."

I hold her fear and rage, as I have often done for my family. I speak to her as gently as I can. She breaks down completely, relating how overworked the nurses are, that they have little time to spend with patients, sick and dying alone in their rooms. "That's not the kind of nurse I am. That's not the way I work." She spends extra time with the patients who reach out to her anyway, ignoring the admonitions of her charge nurse to hurry up and spend less time in each room.

Her distress shakes me. After the session, I cannot engage with Jim or talk at all. I go outside and lie on the grass. I let the emotion drain from me into the earth. I breathe deeply and think of the randomness and unfairness of it all. And I wonder what life will look like when, and if, this ever ends. Will we choose to spend more time at home with our families and those we love, cooking meals and working from home as we did in the 1800s? Will we read more and spend more time conversing, less time working feverishly, and worrying about the status of our hair, makeup, and abs? Will those who "have" more willingly give to and care for those who "have not?" Will we have learned anything from this, our forced journey home and into ourselves? I desperately hope so.

Chapter 21

The Gift of Rain

Ｏne morning I awaken from a dream, elated.

I have been to breakfast with Jim on a Saturday morning. Old friends are coming from out of town for a visit. They are scheduled to arrive at 11:30. After breakfast, I realize that I have just enough time to do some errands in Pasadena and get back home in time to meet our friends, Chris and Kevin.

While walking down Colorado Boulevard, the main drag of Pasadena, I peer into the open door of a large, unfamiliar, dimly lit room. Scuffed round brown tables litter the space. People mingle and drink. At the front of the room, a Caucasian man in his fifties, ill-shaven and dressed in worn crinkled corduroys and an old denim jacket, reads from a book. He beckons me into the darkened space. I recognize him as a famous author whose book, The Gift of Rain, I have just finished reading. I can't believe my good fortune to have happened upon this particular author, reading this particular book, at this particular time. I take a seat and listen. Occasionally, someone passes around a joint, and I breathe it in deeply. The weed elevates me. I am surprised, as weed usually depresses me. Over and over, I think about how happy I am to be there.

Suddenly I look down at my watch and realize it is 1:42. Oh my God, I think. I have been listening to the author for over three hours! And I have totally missed Chris and Kevin waiting for me at my house. But I don't care. This has been worth it. As I leave, the author follows me, asking when he will see me again. I cheerfully tell him I will see him again tomorrow, hoping to return with Jim. "I won't be here tomorrow," he responds, "They're shutting us down." I continue walking down the street, looking for my car, still high from the reading and the weed.

When I get home, Jim tells me that Chris and Kevin never arrived.

In my waking life, I think about the gifts born of this dark, rain-soaked pandemic time. I think of my joy in finding the author within myself, in that dimly lit room, unexpectedly and happily getting high rather than obligatorily meeting with old friends. I am aware that these opportunities for long solitary excursions into creative adventures may not exist tomorrow, next week, or ever again.

I realize the importance of experiencing every moment that greets me, every moment of every day. Tomorrow may not only not exist in this way; it may not exist at all. Wars, genocide, pandemics, and accidents of fate come unbidden and rob us of the world we thought we had and knew. They robbed millions of Armenians of their very lives and denied others, including my grandparents, of the lives their families had known for centuries, They could also rob us of ours.

I feel grateful to have been able to appreciate the gifts of rain.

On Easter Sunday, that day of rebirth and renewal, Alicia finally visits after five weeks of isolation in her Highland Park apartment. She sits on our front porch, a black cotton mask stretched snugly over her mouth and nose. She smiles as we gather the groceries we've ordered for her: vegan cheese, pasta, marinara sauce, bagels, oranges, avocados, and cucumbers. She eagerly devours the vegetable lentil soup I prepared for her while Jim and I feast on roasted turkey breast and lemon meringue pie.

We sit eating and talking at opposing ends of the red brick porch. The rain pelts rhythmically down upon the grass before us. Then, as the grey sun sets, Alicia gets up to leave. Maintaining our social distance, I bow to her, cross my hands across my chest in a hug, and blow her a kiss.

For the previous three weeks, my friend Kim has been forwarding daily updates on Michael, who is still ventilated at our community hospital. One day there's a setback, and his fever spikes; the next, his oxygen levels and breathing improve, and they make plans to remove him from the ventilator. Then his chest fills with liquid, and they keep him on the vent. The day after, they allow his wife and two children, who have recovered from Covid, to visit. His numbers improve dramatically, and the family rejoices. He opens his eyes and seems to communicate.

One day up, the next down, a roller coaster of dread and anxiety tempered with bouts of hope and exhilaration. A roller coaster I know all too well, from tending to sick family members for decades. A roller coaster I'm sure my grandparents also knew only too well as they were forced to leave their ancestral homes and emigrate to a new, unknown world.

Then, a second pneumonia takes hold in Michael's lungs, and then a third, side effects from so many days on the ventilator. Then comes the final missive from Kim:

> *Michael had a very peaceful transition late this morning. His lungs and heart could not take anymore and gave out. Claire and Jason, his son, were with him. They both said how very peaceful he looked. The medical team (doctors and nurses) who have cared for Michael from the beginning cried with Claire and Jason and told them that they have gotten attached to Michael and his family like no other. It was a wonderful tribute.*

The next day the physician who had been by his side for the previous month posted on Instagram:

> *It's been a dark week, lots of loss, lots of grief. I stood at the bedside of a dear patient yesterday, accompanying his family through his last breaths. I'll never forget what his wife said: "It's time to shine your light somewhere else. It burned so bright here." Her beautiful words reminded me that we are all full of light that we can't often see or appreciate. What a gift that his wife and family truly SAW the light within him. . . . I remember that grief is part of loving someone so deeply and reminding myself that it shines elsewhere when our light in this lifetime fades. It's never actually dark. We are never actually lost.*

Michael's death stays with me, lingering below the surface of my daily life, a dull ache. On my daily walks, I am aware of the quiet solemnity emanating from his house around the corner with the four cars in the driveway. Now they will only need three. I wonder what they will do with the fourth. Then I chastise myself for this ridiculous thought.

One day in meditation, Michael appears, hovering above his family, watching, as if trying to make contact with them. I approach him gently and ask if he'd like to move onward toward the light. "No," he says, "I'm not ready yet. I want to stay here a bit longer." I nod and move away from the scene, leaving him in peace.

A week later, a Greek Orthodox church in Pasadena livestreams Michael's funeral from a chapel adorned with Greco-Christian icons: Christ on the Cross and baby Jesus sitting in the arms of the mother, Mary. I count the backs of the heads of six or eight family members in the chapel, masked, huddled in groups of two or three, each group separated by at least six feet. Three eight-foot-high sprays of white and red heart-shaped flowers tower over the chestnut casket, strewn with white lilies, roses, and mums. A smiling photo of Michael resting in an elevated wire frame looks out upon the scene.

Michael's brother sits alone amidst the fifty or sixty chairs lined up in rows of ten before the altar. For what seems like an eternity, two caftan-draped, mustachioed priests pace back and forth in front of the tiny crowd, chanting unenthusiastically in a tongue I can only assume is Greek. They stop now and then to cross themselves, forehead to sternum, left breast to right breast. The onlookers follow, genuflecting silently.

The younger priest quotes a Bible verse from the wooden lectern. Finally, the elder of the two utters a few words about Michael in a sedate monotone, hardly looking up from his notes. In the front row, Claire sniffles into her handkerchief.

I wait to be moved, to feel the essence of Michael, for a family member to give a eulogy or say a few words, to feel an emotion commensurate with the experience. It never comes. Only more chanting, more sniffling, and silence. I turn off my computer and sit silently, sad at how life has been laid bare and denuded, void of music, heart, and celebration, during the pandemic.

One day last week, on my trek around the block, I spy two ambling walkers, one six or eight feet in front of the other, slowly approaching. As they draw nearer, I recognize the elderly Korean couple outfitted in bright yellow zip-up sweatshirts today. I wave strenuously, feeling my face crease into a colossal smile. "How are you?" I almost yell across the fifteen-foot chasm that separates us. I ask, having no idea if they understand me. They return my wide smile, eyes twinkling: "One month. Stay inside. We're old," they grin. I say how happy I am to see them, noting the gaunt paleness of their faces against the brightness of their hoodies. They gently chuckle in return. Had they been sick, I wonder, or just playing it safe?

I feel my heart burst with happiness at this one return to normal, and I bounce my way down the rest of the block.

Chapter 22

On Depression

I jolt awake in the middle of the night, terrified as the bed shakes and rocks beneath me. I want to get up and run outside, fearful that this is the "Big One" we Californians have awaited for decades.

"No, stay here," Jim admonishes. He flips furtively through his phone for news. "It's okay. It's stopped; it's only a 4.7 on the Richter scale."

But terror constricts my chest, and I lie there, waiting for the next jolt. It feels like I lie there taut in my bed for an hour, externally frozen but internally shaking.

I don't recognize this response in myself. A native Californian, I've lived through numerous earthquakes in my life, much more powerful than this, without fear. I'm surprised—why this response now?

But this night feels different. We'd heard that Ruth Bader Ginsburg, the liberal firebrand Supreme Court justice, had died the afternoon before, making way for President Donald Trump to appoint his third conservative justice to the Supreme Court in three and a half years. Roe v. Wade, gun control, the Affordable Care Act, and environmental issues near and dear to my heart now become seriously threatened.

RBG's death the day before had shaken me even more than this earthquake. While ill for a long time, Justice Ginsburg had seemed like the proverbial cat with nine lives, beating cancer many times. Many of us had prayed she'd remain healthy until we could vote Trump out of office.

But no such luck. So now I shake not only from the terror of the earthquake and the worldwide pandemic still killing thousands of people daily, but the increasing terror of what might become our country.

Grey, billowy smoke still hangs over the long swath of California, carpeting our cars with a layer of silver ash, a blanket of smoke with no end, stretching from the heavens into the deep crevices of the earth. Again, no exit. Nowhere to go. Nowhere to escape. The fires rage from the eastern borders of Washington, down through Oregon, and along the entire California coast. Millions of acres have burned, dozens of people have perished, and hundreds of thousands have been evacuated.

Apocalypse upon apocalypse upon apocalypse. First, the pandemic, which continues to flourish, and now the fires that keep us even further indoors than the virus. At least with the virus, we could walk and run outside. Now the smoke stings our eyes and chokes our lungs. If I venture out, I do so with an N95 mask tightened against my nose and mouth. A mask that I'm not supposed to have, ordered months ago to donate to a local hospital or fire station.

A layer of guilt placed upon the blanket of ash.

This virus, and perhaps now the fires, the earthquakes, and our perilous political situation, throw us back upon ourselves, calling us to face our innermost beings. Devoid of our usual distractions, those who pay attention have no choice but to grapple with who we are and where we come from.

I watch the ways depression drops in on me from time to time, enveloping me in its cold embrace, rising unbidden when I least expect it, knocking on dawn's door. I think of that little girl in the big house in Altadena. I know she was often depressed, a sensitive person who felt everything too deeply and could read the light or discordant energy in every room. She ate, read, climbed into avocado trees, and escaped to friends' houses to medicate the feelings that threatened to overwhelm her. How much was hers, this pain, this depression, and how much passed down from her grandparents and her parents, hidden, denied trauma coursing through DNA? What did she carry that others could not bear to acknowledge?

As a grownup, the little girl utilized more sophisticated forms of medication for her depression: work, book groups, artists' groups, women's groups, and meditation groups, not to mention therapy and, at times, actual medication. Now, during this unprecedented time, many of these grown-up medications have been whisked away, and the angry dragon of depression rears her head and demands to be heard. The twisting in the belly, the rage in the gut, the fear in the heart—they loom up, sometimes pouring out inappropriately on Jim or keeping me up at night, alternately seething and crying.

Maybe it's all been just a way to medicate the depression, I wonder, all that overachieving: the advanced degrees, the people-pleasing, the committees, and scholarships, and all the rest—just a way to manage that core depression in whatever ways I could.

When left to my own devices, when something takes away the work and all the people, and the meetings and the distractions, I am sometimes left with sadness and grief. Sadness at the lost friends, the deceased parents, the end of child-rearing, the people dying alone in coronavirus wards, the firefighters fighting unrelenting blazes, the thousands displaced and losing their homes, and our terrible political situation with Donald Trump at the helm. Not to mention the unacknowledged and unbearable sadness of what happened to my ancestors decades ago.

Sometimes, I want to crawl into myself, curl tightly into the fetal position, and tuck into my womb. As Wordsworth says, "The world is too much with us," and I want to hide from it. I want to hide not only from the world but from my own emotions. But I don't know where to run.

I think of Rumi's poem "The Guest House," and know that I'm facing a new arrival, a rather unwelcome visitor. She smacks me in the face with her sudden weeping, aches in the heart, and unbidden anger. I want her gone. I do not want to welcome her in, as Rumi suggests I should. I have always wanted her gone, medicating her early on with bowls of ice cream and stolen cookies, ministering to friends and family, any way to escape the self. Later, I even found a way to get paid for this ministration, this latter form of medication. A wise therapist friend once said that if we were really healthy, would we continue to do this work of ministering to others? I've pondered that question for decades.

While I still wish the depression gone, I know now to engage it, speak with it, and see what it wants to teach me. "All is not well," it says to me. "You are a lightning rod for what lies around you." And now, all is not well with me. I have uncovered the deep, dark blanket lying at the base of my soul. I want to dissolve it and see its particles drift off into the ozone, like the specks of grey ash outside my window.

But it serves a purpose. "Go deeper," it says. "Sink deeper. You carry the darkness of generations of trampled-upon people. Healing only happens at that level. No number of accomplishments, accolades, friends, chocolate bars, or traveling can dissipate what lies at the core."

Jim and I have set up an uneasy truce, traipsing our laptops and phones from one room to another and from the front porch to the back, talking with our respective clients on Zoom or FaceTime. I'm not sure we've spent this much uninterrupted time together in our 34 years of marriage. Our mutual love of independence brought us together. In the early days, he'd head off alone to the desert in his Land Cruiser, driving over dirt roads and hanging out in natural hot springs. Later, he'd spend weeks in Peru and Chile leading mountain-climbing trips or jungle excursions to partake of plant medicines. On the other hand, I would travel to monasteries and retreat houses to study with monks, theologians, and psychologists. Now we navigate around each other and the colorful Adirondack chairs spaced throughout our yard, meeting every night for dinner to catch up on the day's events.

I miss seeing my clients in person. I even miss hugging them. After all these years of practice, I am one of those therapists who hugs the clients who reach out to me. I miss hugging my friends too. I appreciate that I sometimes see them masked and socially distanced on our long walks around the neighborhood, but I want to embrace them and feel their warmth and aliveness against my own.

My sister and her husband have agreed to go away with us for a few days to celebrate my 65th birthday. Can I hug this sister whom I haven't seen in months? Can we eat together indoors? Need we get tested first and wear masks? These ridiculous questions raise their ugly heads again as things inch toward opening up here in California. I still hate these questions. They make me want to cry.

Alicia tries to soothe me. She says, of course, you feel bad. We all feel bad. She has surrendered to this time of isolation, accepted it as temporary, and can sit with it. I want to get away from it, run from it. She is younger and wiser.

Stop and face yourself, I say to myself. The opportunity for deep healing presents itself if you allow her in. I don't want to feel bad anymore. I've been running from my depression all these years. I tell myself, stop. Face her. Confront her. Learn what she has to teach.

So what does she wish to say?

"Pay attention to me." That's what she's saying.

"Pay attention to me," like that little girl always wanted to say but never dared to. "Pay attention to me," like my daughter whines with a twinkle in her eye, her hands hugging her shoulders. Only she can say it. And I laugh and cock my head to gaze at her, smiling.

I could not say it. I didn't know how. I only knew that I hurt.

So okay, I tell Depression, I'm paying attention. I'm all ears. I'm listening. What more do you want?

"I exist. I want to be seen. I want you to acknowledge me."

It has never been lost on me that I went into this field of psychology to give others what I have personally craved.

But the depression has served another function, of course. A portal to other worlds to find its healing: the worlds of books, the worlds of ideas, the worlds of different cultures, the worlds of psychology and spirituality, and most of all, the worlds of mystery I cannot see but only sense.

In desperation, I let go. I surrender. I stop resisting. I breathe deeply. I engage the solitude.

With every breath, my stomach relaxes, my heart beats more slowly, and the rage in my chest subsides. I ask whomever, whatever, is out there for help. On good days, a blanket of calm replaces the cloak of darkness. Light opens within and the heavens open above, sprinkling peace over me like a vodka and tonic without the hangover.

Depression throws me back upon myself, which in turn throws me back upon the transcendent. And maybe that was the design, after all. To throw me back upon what matters most: the mystery, the unseen, the other worlds we sense but can't know. And for that, I am grateful to that roaring purple dragon that comes unbidden to knock at my door.

On this mild late September day, I sit perched on my front porch reading Dennis Patrick Slattery's *Grace in the Desert*, describing his three-month journey to spiritual retreat centers throughout the western United States. Like many other spiritual seekers, he talks about the necessity of solitude to point us toward the Divine. I watch the yellow butterflies dart, and the hummingbirds flap their wings above the clear glass feeder. My soul is hungry. Hungry for beauty, nature, and most of all, for the solitude of the Self. Ironic that in this time of sheltering in place, I should crave the solitude of nature outside my door. But I spend too much time hovering over computer screens or cradling my tiny iPhone.

Every Tuesday, Thursday, and Saturday morning at 7:30 a.m., I gulp down my hot tea and sleepily reach for my computer to flick on Mynoo's morning meditation, miraculously appearing on my laptop from her 6 p.m. brightly lit opalescent walls in Mumbai, India. Amethyst and quartz crystals scatter on the bookshelves behind her, and the abstract painting's vibrant reds, blues, and purples on the wall above peer over her shoulder.

We chant what she calls "The Global Human Vibe Attunement."

"I Acknowledge myself as a Human, I Receive myself as a Human, I Accept myself as a Human."

The chant is designed to anchor the soul into the body at this time. A chant for all of us who feel viscerally like we sometimes don't want to be here and that home is somewhere else rather than on this earth. Somewhere else in a distant, ungraspable memory where this pain of living in the material world isn't so great. A world, I imagine, where genocide and death, war, hatred, famine, and pandemics don't exist.

While I often feel foolish repeating these words aloud with a woman from India thousands of miles away whom I hardly know, I do so nonetheless, relishing the peace and calm that envelops me after each session. So I continue to chant: "I Acknowledge myself as a Human. I Receive myself as a Human. I Accept myself as a Human."

I welcome my soul into my body, as I have welcomed Depression into my psyche, mining its riches to see what new insights and delights it offers.

Chapter 23

Artsakh and Hagia Sofia

J im and I cruise around the neighborhood on a sunset jaunt, our
nightly ritual to get out of the house after a long day tethered to laptops and iPhones. I notice unfamiliar orange and peacock-blue signs
littering our community's front lawns and sidewalks.

"Peace to Artsakh" and "We Stand With Artsakh" jumps out in
bold, red lettering against dramatic orange backgrounds. The large
signs dwarf the "Biden/Harris for President" signs joining them this
week before the contentious 2020 elections. Large pictures of a man's
face with "Fascist" splayed across it stare at us from telephone poles
near busy intersections. Underneath the picture is the man's name,
"Erdogan," Turkey's current president.

Eight by ten-inch cotton flags, in the same bold colors and attached to foot-long sticks, fly from car windows whizzing down Foot-
hill Boulevard., the main drag of our Los Angeles suburb. A month
before, I had not seen or recognized these blue, orange, and red flags.
Now, these flags representing the Republic of Artsakh, a historically
Armenian stronghold, appear everywhere. I examine the signs and the
banners with curiosity.

I receive daily Instagram posts from Pari, now 25, the eldest of the
children from the Long Island Armenian family on the Genocide Tour.
Pari and I had sat in the back of that white Mercedes van, sharing stories of her college life. Now, five years later, Pari attends Harvard Law
School after having completed a Master's degree in Human Rights at

Columbia University. She messages me the articles she's written for a Columbia human rights periodical and a law blog titled *LawFare* about the situation in Artsakh. She's educating the uneducated, including myself, about the present war between Armenia and Azerbaijan.

My Armenian client Taline calls sobbing, telling me she can't sleep at night and has trouble concentrating on her work because of the war. Her older brother Alex, now in his late 40s with a wife and two sons, has made reservations to fly to Yerevan, the capital of Armenia, to fight against the Azeris, as he did in the 1992 war between Armenia and Azerbaijan. Though he now has severe back trouble and, according to Taline, carries an extra forty or fifty pounds, he refuses to sit idly by. At the same time, thousands of Armenians from the international diaspora are arriving to fight in Artsakh. More than a thousand soldiers and 30 civilians have already perished in the cease-fire broken by Azerbaijan after 26 years of relative peace.

I hear Taline's pain, and I am speechless. I do not understand her devotion. I do not feel the deep, personal angst that she and her family are experiencing. This war feels far, far away from my comfortable life, even during the pandemic. Since the border was closed during my Genocide Tour, I have never set foot in modern Armenia, have no relatives there, and know no one who lives there. This war strikes me as just another violent skirmish covered on the fifth page of the *LA Times*, like so many other violent skirmishes that break out worldwide. A skirmish that has nothing to do with me. To Taline, however, it's as if the Azeri army has stormed her Southern California town and is breaking down her back door.

Yet this particular altercation does have something to do with me, though I have trouble feeling the immensity of it. Turkey has supplied the Azerbaijani troops with drones and munitions to fight against the Armenians. "They've set out to complete what they started with the genocide," Alex warns Taline. "They want to finish us off." This echoes Turkish President Erdogan's recent proclamation: "[W]e will continue to fulfill the mission our grandfathers have carried out for centuries in the Caucasus"—an indirect reference to the Armenian Genocide carried out by the founders of the Turkish Republic.

These statements chill me. Turkey wants to finish, in 2020, the extermination of the Armenians they began in 1895. I find it surreal and unbelievable.

It is unclear how long the fighting can go on with such uneven resources. Armenia and Artsakh provide a home to just over 3 million people, outnumbered 30-to-1 by the combined population of Azerbaijan (10 million) and Turkey (83 million.)

The Armenians, all Christian, and the Azerbaijanis, 96% Shia Muslim, have been at odds for decades fighting over this independent region, the Republic of Nagorno-Karabagh, called Artsakh by Armenians. Nagorno-Karabagh nestles between the two countries of Armenia and Azerbaijan. Artsakh has been populated mainly by Armenians for centuries but is internationally recognized as belonging to Azerbaijan, having been ceded to Azerbaijan during the Stalin Area.

I take a deep dive into whatever research I can find about the region of Artsakh and learn that it occupies a space no bigger than the state of Delaware and hosts a population of around 150,000 people, almost all ethnically Armenian. It sees itself as a de facto independent republic with its own parliament, president, and army.

I learn that after the fall of the Soviet Union in 1991, the Armenians, unwilling to give up their historic homeland, fought the Azeris to win back the land they felt was rightfully theirs. During that war, Armenia succeeded in driving 600,000 Azerbaijanis from their homes. Now the Azeris want to reclaim these lands. Skirmishes lasting a few days have broken out since the ceasefire brokered in 1994 between the two countries, but nothing like this current war.

Here in Southern California, Armenian protestors rise, blocking major thoroughfares and closing busy freeways. Tens of thousands from this largest Armenian diaspora in the world march to draw attention to this situation many thousands of miles away that once again, as in 1915, threatens the very existence of the Armenian people. Armenians worldwide are acutely aware that aid from the international community, from the French and the Americans, was too little too late to help them one hundred years ago. They fear history is repeating itself now.

As my mind tries to focus on the details of the war, I'm reminded of an experience I had several months before. The words "Hagia Sophia" caught my eye when I flipped through the Sunday *LA Times* World Section. I yanked the page open, wondering what the *LA Times* might say about this church in Istanbul.

Recently, I'd been eyeing the glossy Hagia Sophia tourist book I'd bought at the kiosk outside the Istanbul monument on the first day of my Genocide Tour, the only such book I'd bought in decades. Daily, I trudged past the bookshelf on my path from the bedroom through the den to the kitchen, its bright sapphire cover gathering dust, unopened on that shelf for five years. How many times had I intended to open the guidebook and experience once again the majesty of Hagia Sophia?

I encountered Hagia Sophia on my first day in Istanbul. I'd arrived the day before I had to meet the rest of my tour and had been introduced to Salpi, one of the other single women on the trip. Salpi and I walked around the old town of Istanbul, stopping at an open food bazaar to gawk at the brightly colored spice shops, littered with varying shades of red pepper and orange saffron, deep green dried mint, and ochre cardamon pods. Nuts of every color, size, and shape beckoned from large white bins, as mustachioed vendors offered samples of their wares. Freshly caught, slimy fish stared out at us, displayed in shallow pans of water, as massive, red spiced sausages hung like giant sea slugs from the ceilings of the food stalls.

Salpi and I had taken a bus tour around the city, and a boat ride through the Bosporus. I had waited to be entranced by the canals and the blue sea, the spice markets, and the calls to prayer, but nothing touched me. I'd gone through the day as if in a fog, unmoved by the surroundings. Finally, we stopped at Hagia Sophia.

The monument was originally built as a Christian cathedral in the 6th century and converted to a mosque by the Ottoman Empire during their reign. In 1936, UNESCO designated Hagia Sophia as a museum and a UNESCO World Heritage Site, attracting visitors worldwide as a "monument to all of mankind . . . a symbol of solidarity among all religions."

I remember approaching the massive cluster of unadorned, grey and ochre stone buildings of various sizes and shapes, stretching over many acres which made up Hagia Sophia. The cathedral complex occupied an outcropping of land bordered on three sides by the sparkling blue Sea of Marmara. Four slender minarets shot high into the sky, forming a square of blue amidst the amalgam of buildings.

Eyeing the mass of structures before us and wilting from the long hot day, Salpi and I blindly followed the hordes of tourists walking toward the entrance through gardens of lush purple and pink flowers and manicured green hedges. The cathedral's size overwhelmed me as I entered the ornate front gates. Huge black discs with indecipherable gold Islamic script hung alongside ancient frescoes and mosaics of Jesus, Mary, and the apostles. Black and grey painted angels stared out from the crevices high above the center of the nave, competing for attention with the ornate, inlaid ivory Islamic fences overlaying the walls.

Centuries upon centuries of civilizations laid one on top of another.

I stopped in front of a half-restored fresco of Jesus flanked by two apostles. The ancient pale figures mesmerized me. I felt my heart open, enveloped in an oasis of calm amidst the cacophony of the monument, taking picture after picture in front of the three twenty-foot figures, the eyes of Jesus boring down upon me. The angels, Mary, and another depiction of Jesus stared down from the cathedral dome. Blocking out the tourists and the looming black discs, the figures called out to me, making me feel deeply at home. As this was my first day in Turkey, I had not yet realized that most of the churches there had been transformed into mosques, and that this would be the first of very few times I would experience any trace of the faith of my ancestors in my ancestral homeland.

Now, according to the article in the *LA Times*, Erdogan, the despotic ruler of Turkey, had mandated that Hagia Sofia be converted into a mosque after almost eighty years as a monument to all faiths and religions. My heart shrank with disbelief as I read the article. I stopped reading, stunned. Some unconscious ancestral attachment within me recoiled at the thought of yet another extinguishing of my faith by Turkey and all that the Armenians lived and died for.

As tears streamed down my face, I fumbled to explain to my befuddled husband and daughter what it meant to have Hagia Sofia, a place they'd never heard of, made into a mosque. I tried to explain the transgenerational tears of yet another loss to the Christian Armenian people. Jim and Alicia, largely unfamiliar with and disinterested in anything Armenian, peered at me quizzically, looking from one to the other, seeking an understanding of my strange behavior.

I retreated to my bedroom to re-read the article and to integrate this new information in solitude.

Though raised in the Presbyterian Church, I've hardly been devoted. I worry that I'm considered a heretic by many of my more conservative Armenian relatives for my acceptance of forms of spirituality other than Christianity. Yet Christianity courses through my veins, as it does through the blood of all Armenians. None of us has escaped hearing that the Armenians represent the first Christian nation, adopting Christianity in 301 AD, and that Noah's Ark reputedly landed on the banks of Mt. Ararat. This grief at the transformation of Hagia Sophia both startled me and made sense, as I'd come to embrace my Armenian heritage more and more during the five years since I visited her.

I have always felt at home in churches, though it's been months, maybe years, since I've sat inside one. Within their walls, "The peace that surpasses all understanding" often visits me and connects me to something sacred, no matter where I am.

Once, in a healing exercise designed to clear karma from past lives, I was taken back to a life in which I had been a greying Russian priest, living at the back of a crumbling Catholic church, hobbling to greet every visitor, while crossing myself with aged, feeble fingers. The regression helped me understand my peculiar attraction to Catholic rituals, with which I have not been raised but have always resonated deeply within me. As a child, I yearned to accompany my best friend to the Catholic church across the street from my family's Presbyterian church. I wanted to kneel and take the communion bread and wine into my mouth. I yearned to wear a long white dress and gold cross and walk down the church's center aisle to receive my first communion as my best friend had.

———————————

Some say this present war between Armenia and Azerbaijan is about oil and money, like so many wars, not about faith and culture. But I'm not so sure. This particular attempt at ethnic cleansing, like so many others, must arise from some more profound, more threatening terror of the Other. A terror so deep that annihilation seems the only solution.

I have read that in Turkey before the genocide, the Armenians, who had been considered compliant, second-class citizens because of their Christian faith, began to rise up and demand reforms. They sought equal taxation, having been taxed almost double that of Turks, and additional rights that had been denied them because of their ethnicity. Becoming ever more successful due to the reforms, they became a threat not only to the Ottomans' faith but to their very way of life.

I also learned that in the early years of World War I, the Turks encouraged the Turkish Armenians fighting for the Turkish army to incite their Armenian counterparts fighting for Russia to rise against Russia, Turkey's enemy. The Turks wanted to win back lands seized by Russia in the Russo-Turkish War of 1877-1878. When Russian armies roundly defeated the Turks in 1914, the Turks blamed the Armenians for siding with the Russians.

The Armenians became the "inner enemy" within their borders, a people upon whom to project the Turks' shadow of failure and defeat.

At the time, Turkish Ottoman propaganda described Armenians as "traitors, saboteurs, spies, conspirators, vermin, and infidels." In February 1915, Nazım Bey, one of the Young Turks masterminds of the genocide, argued that "it is absolutely necessary to eliminate the Armenian people in its entirety so that there is no further Armenian on this earth and the very concept of Armenia is extinguished." The idea was promoted that "Turkey could only be revitalized if it rid itself of its non-Muslim elements."

As before, the Armenians now threaten the Azeris with their very existence on their historic land. The fight is not only for money, land, power, and the right to worship as one pleases, but for existence itself.

While I have trouble feeling the full horror of this war over a patch of land I've never stood upon, as Taline and her family feel, I feel deeply the loss of the ancient church that welcomed me to Istanbul and helped me feel at home in a land to which my people no longer belong.

Now, in Artsakh, Armenians fight once again to continue to live on land they have inhabited for almost four centuries. They fight to retain what little remains of their land, culture, and history. For a people who have lost so much, this fight represents no less than life over death and the continuity of an ancient tribe.

———

Later, as I read the latest news from the front in Nagorno-Karabagh, I learned that Russian President Vladimir Putin had brokered another cease-fire between Armenia and Azerbaijan. The Azerbaijanis have captured the town of Shushi, one of the major centers of Armenian life in Artsakh. The road from Armenia to Shushi, the Lachin Corridor, has also been captured, making it impossible for Armenians to send military troops and support to their fighting

comrades. Shushi has been turned over to Azerbaijan, and Azeri refugees exiled by the Armenians in the 1992 war have been invited to
repatriate these lands.

Riots have broken out in Yerevan, protesting this cease-fire. I hear
Armenians the world over weeping at this loss. Though relieved that
no more lives will be lost, at least for now, and that this horrible war
will cease, I feel the silent pain reverberating throughout the Armenian
diaspora and within my heart for all the lives, both Armenian and Azerbaijani, lost. And I feel an even greater ache that, once again, our little
tribe has been beaten back.

Now, as Jim and I traverse the streets around our neighborhood,
relieving the anxiety of these long pandemic days, I have an increased
understanding of what these "We Stand with Artsakh" signs
mean. Not only what they mean to the Armenian culture, but to me
personally. This war and this time of unprecedented contemplation
and sheltering-in-place have deepened my sense not only of myself as
an Armenian, but of the ways in which trauma, however large or
small, seeps into our souls and transforms us. I watch the way depression rears her angry head within me, both in response to our present
situation, and as a possible remnant of those long-ago days in Turkey.
I also watch the ways in which this pandemic robs so many of their
loved ones, as the genocide did over a hundred years ago in Turkey.

In contrast, I also appreciate more fully the unutterable beauty of
nature, even in these worst of times, and the space to embrace the
ordinary pleasures of our days. I understand more deeply the faith
structures which sustain me and have sustained my people since the
beginning of time. I only hope that these structures also sustain the
millions that suffer throughout the world, either from this pandemic
or from the wars that rage within it.

SECTION FOUR

Finding the Mandorla

*The mandorla binds together that which was torn apart and
made unwhole—unholy.*

~Robert Johnson

In the years following the Genocide Tour and through the pandemic,
moments of integration and healing arose spontaneously and unbidden.

In dreams, at family funerals and weddings, and through experiences with indigenous plant medicines and local healers, I touched the holy center of the mandorla. In those moments of awe, I felt the full embrace of my familial and ancestral heritage, joining together my Armenian and American selves. I found answers to the question, which initially brought me to this journey, "What does healing look like, and how do we forgive our perpetrators?" These chapters point to that holy integration of those two worlds within my soul.

Chapter 24

The Funeral

Jim, Alicia, and I sprawl, limbs intertwined, on the overstuffed couches in our darkened living room. The smell of the cinnamon candles left over from Christmas permeates the evening as the fire crackles before us. We have decided to play hooky and stay home this New Year's Eve. We have made excuses for the various parties to which we have been invited. Alicia feels too tired to drive across LA to meet her friend Chloe, and Jim and I prefer a quiet evening at home to the cocktails and small talk party down the street.

Instead, we sit together laughing, playing a new word game Alicia has picked up, and eating Indian food around the warmth of the leaping flames. We take turns blowing our intentions for the New Year into toothpicks and throwing them into the fire. Suddenly, my phone rings from the kitchen. Who is calling me at 9 p.m. on New Year's Eve? I wonder. The name "Narine" glows on the iPhone screen. Ahh, my old country cousin who calls several times a year to bring the good news that "He is Risen" (Happy Easter) or "Bless this day of His birth" (Merry Christmas.) She must be calling to wish me Happy New Year, and I let the call go to voicemail. Then I stop, remembering that Narine's mother has been ill. I worry that perhaps she is calling to tell me that her mother has died.

I press my voicemail and hear Narine's strained, accented voice confirm that her mother has "gone to be with the Lord." I call her back immediately. "I'm so sorry to hear that your dear mother has passed on, Narine."

She replies curtly. "She didn't pass on. She has gone to be with the Lord."

I correct myself. "I'm so sorry she has gone to be with the Lord."

Like many of my immigrant Armenian cousins, Narine appears to practice a more conservative brand of Christianity than I do. I have often feared her judgment of the openness with which I have raised Alicia, exposing her to Buddhism, Hinduism, Shamanism, and various forms of meditation. Perhaps to Narine, this acceptance of other faiths affronts the very essence of what it means to be Armenian and betrays all that she and our ancestors have fought and suffered for. Not only do I not speak Armenian or attend an Armenian church, but I believe that many paths, in addition to Christianity, lead toward the Divine.

My cousins schedule their mother's funeral for the following Friday, my first Friday back from the Christmas break. My client schedule is packed to the gills that week, as usual for a week after a vacation. I struggle with where to reschedule the clients and whether to attend the funeral. I feel concerned about disrupting my heavy work schedule, but I know it's important that at least one of the four siblings in my family attend the funeral.

My siblings and I have a complicated relationship with these cousins from Syria. At least I have a complex relationship with these cousins. Narine and her younger sister Ovsanna are close in age to me. They relocated from Aleppo in their late teens to "be with family." Their three uncles had emigrated to Los Angeles years before, and Narine's mom, the oldest of the four siblings, wanted to join them here. They had told me of their happy childhoods in Aleppo, that they had not come to California willingly and had been disappointed once here. Although they came here to "be with family," Ovsanna once told me that she felt that her family had often not been there for them. She felt that she hardly saw her cousins. I knew I was included in that group she hardly saw and had always felt bad about that.

I had my American life and friends and hadn't known how to integrate these newly arrived Armenian cousins into my world. When Narine called to wish me Happy Easter or Merry Christmas, she prefaced the call half-jokingly with, "This is Narine. You remember me, don't you? I am your cousin." Message received, I would think, a leaden ball of guilt twisting in my gut. So it felt important to attend her mother's funeral, no matter how difficult it might be to cancel a day's worth of clients and motor across Los Angeles in hellish Friday morning traffic.

Fortuitously, I arrive early at the low-lying white church with black Armenian lettering scrawled across its facade. I sit alone toward the back, the better to observe the scene before me. Eight gargantuan rainbow-colored arrangements of flowers line the front of the altar, dramatic against the white of the church. Several are shaped into white crosses, and three display red and pink chrysanthemum hearts splayed with banners reading "Beloved Grandmother," "Beloved Sister," and "Beloved Mother."

I have never seen so many exquisite flower arrangements at one funeral. After a while, the deceased's younger brother, my second cousin, and his wife arrive, sitting in one of the front pews. He motions me to join him. Though happy with my solo seat toward the back, I take my place next to my cousin, grateful that he has included me and not wanting to disappoint him. I watch silently as rows and rows of black-clad people enter the church with somber looks, many with tear-stained cheeks. It becomes clear that this is no modern American "Celebration of Life"—this is a funeral meant for mourning—no white, red, or even blue hues spring from the clothing of the mourners. I become acutely conscious of the bright red vest I wear over my cream-colored silk blouse.

The church is now a sea of black suits, black hair, and black eyes. I recognize almost no one, which is fine with me, the better to observe the unfolding experience. Soon, I realize that none of my three siblings are coming, each having texted a different excuse for their absence. A couple of the priests, the four Der Hayrs, pace back and forth in their long black robes and tall pointed black hats, swinging miters of incense throughout the church. Finally, one of the priests starts chanting Armenian in a sing-song voice, his mournful utterances floating above the pews alongside the incense smoke.

I assume this is the Armenian version of the Jewish cantor. I have no idea what he is saying. Now and then, I hear the one word I recognize: the mournful prayer "Dervormia." *Lord have mercy.* "Dervormia, Dervormia," over and over. In a whisper, I ask my cousin where Narine and Ovsanna are. He points to the front row where Narine sits, head bent, lustrous black hair pulled severely back from her pale white forehead, dark sunglasses only partially shielding the deep black circles under her eyes. She wears baggy black pants and an oversized black sweater. I hardly recognize her. She has become frail and waif-like since the last time I saw her. A woman with bleached blonde hair and a black beret sits beside her, weeping. I realize it is Ovsanna, who has come to resemble her mother in the few years since I've last seen her.

I am brought out of my focus on Ovsanna when the eldest priest begins speaking Armenian at the podium. It dawns on me that this service will be conducted in Armenian. Oh no, I think, why hadn't I thought of that? I'm not going to understand a word of this. With a quick look around the church at the nodding heads, I realize I am probably the only one in this group of one hundred-plus who doesn't speak Armenian, save for my cousin's lovely Danish wife who sits next to me. But, as the hour wears on, I sit lulled by the cadence of the language that is both familiar and incomprehensible. After more talk from the priest, several eulogies, and some chanting, people begin to file out, squinting in the noonday sun. I notice Johno, one of the deceased's other brothers, standing at the back of the church alone, gazing at the open coffin in front of the altar. I walk toward him and slip my arm through his. Johno was my first love. Now, here we stand sixty-one years later, arm in arm. I am now 63, and Johno 85.

One of the mourners offers Johno his condolences, and Johno introduces me as "Chuchilik," that old term of endearment. In all these years, nothing has changed between us. We stand together silently for a long while. Then Johno gently murmurs, "They're burying a part of me in that coffin today." My heart breaks to hear how much he will miss his only sister. I am touched beyond words that he has shared this piece of his soul with me. At that moment, I understand why I am here at this funeral, to be present for this man who was so present for me as a child.

Suddenly I hear a loud wail emanate from the small group still clustered around the open coffin at the front of the otherwise empty church. I see arms reaching out like the tentacles of an octopus as the morticians move to close the casket. Agonized screams pierce the quiet. Narine and Ovsanna reach out to hold their younger sister Arsine back as she lunges toward the mahogany coffin as if to join her deceased mother. I have heard of Jewish women wailing at the Western Wall in Jerusalem, but have never witnessed this, let alone in my own family. I watch, a stunned silent witness to my cousin's grief, as new tears begin to soak Johno's cheeks. We turn and leave the church, joining the dark throng gathered on the front steps.

Arsine's dramatic expression of grief shakes me. I'm awed by this public display. I keep peering back into the church to see if she is okay. I feel as if I have stepped into a foreign world, far removed from the pablum of the American Presbyterian church of my youth. I feel transported into my ancestors' Middle Eastern world.

Attending the funeral touched something deep within me. I loved everything about it: the mournful cadences of the chanting, the smell of the wafting incense, the Der Hayrs in their ancient garb, and the expressions of deep, heartfelt emotion. I loved the long wooden tables laden with grape leaves, pita bread, hummus, and rice pilaf that welcomed us after the funeral service, and I loved the endless, laborious prayers spoken in Armenian before the meal.

I have always felt honored in this extended family, though I rarely see them. I have also felt myself lacking and "not enough," as if I always disappoint them, failing to live up to their ideal of what it means to be Armenian. I associate this criticality and not-enoughness with being Armenian. Perhaps I am tapping into what Armenians, continually oppressed, have always felt—"not enough." As a result, I have sometimes sought to distance myself from this often dark, melancholy world with its deep sense of obligation and proscribed social roles.

But at the funeral, I experienced what I had given up for my modern American life. With the tight family structures and the frequent attendance at family functions comes a sense of belonging and community. This sense of belonging comes at a price, to be sure, but I realized how I had been looking for that lost sense of community my entire life. I studied and worked in Italy, Spain, Pakistan, and China in my 20s. I was looking for something—I just never knew what. I was looking for something when I developed a specialty in Cross-Cultural Counseling for my Ph.D. long before learning about other cultures became fashionable.

Reflecting upon my reactions to the funeral, I realized I was looking for "home"—the ancestral home of deep relationships and a sense of a community that would always be there. I became acutely aware of the personal cost of assimilation in a way I had never experienced. In some ways, my parents rejected our familial roots, choosing instead to become "Americans." Like many children of immigrants in their generation, they had succeeded, working hard to attain the American dream and raise an exemplary American family in Southern California. But unbeknownst to me, I had been searching for that left-behind culture my whole life. I found it in the center of the mandorla at my cousin's funeral.

Chapter 25

The Dream of Tom

I jolt wide awake at 3 a.m. I have dreamt of Tom. Two crystal clear images play in my consciousness. I run the pictures over in my mind, attempting to sear them into my memory. I need to remember this dream in the morning. It feels important. Dreams rarely awaken me; when they do, I know to pay attention. I know I should get up and write the dream down immediately. I know my dismal history of remembering my nighttime dreams in the morning. But instead of writing down the dream, I lie still, reviewing the dream image by image in the movie theatre of my mind.

Then suddenly, morning. Only one gleaming image remains of the two.

I am walking alone in a field, the soil overturned but not yet planted. I run into Tom unexpectedly. I see no one else around. His face gleams with pearls of sweat, backlit by the sharp rays of the midday sun. His broad smile lights up the field, with his square-jawed face, black horn-rimmed glasses, and slightly receding hairline moving up from a deeply ridged forehead. He stares at me, saying nothing, only smiling. His tight white t-shirt reveals fieldworker's muscles. A buff, older version of James Dean. His ridged torso looks nothing like the soft white belly of the 21-year-old college senior I had known. He holds a hoe in his arms, ready to till the brown soil beneath him.

I hug Tom over and over. I tell him how overjoyed I am to see him. It feels like coming home, this accidental encounter with Tom, whom I haven't seen or thought about in years.

Then the image fades. What happened next? Did we walk through the field arm in arm, talk about old times, and hug some more? I don't know. The second image had fled.

I was a high school senior when I received a letter from Tom Balikian, a single sheet amidst a huge packet from Colorado College as part of my new student orientation. I didn't read the sheet; I just noticed the "ian" of the Armenian name.

CC is a small, progressive liberal arts school in Colorado Springs. I had never heard of the college before my high school counselor suggested I apply. When I got accepted, he just said, "Go. If you're accepted there, go." Eager to leave Southern California, I sent my regrets to my hometown colleges to go to Colorado, a school I knew nothing about in a place I'd never been.

When I arrived on campus the following fall, I hardly noticed the tall, scruffy senior with wild stringy hair, worn blue jeans caked with dirt, rumpled flannel shirt, and square, black horn-rimmed glasses who lived down the hall from me. One day soon after I moved in, he introduced himself as Tom Balikian. "Hey," I responded, "didn't I get a letter from you? I thought you were a dean or something. How come you sent me a letter?"

"I'm the student body president," he grinned. "I just wanted to introduce myself."

Oh. I thought. That's weird. I thought the Armenian letter was from someone important, not this scruffy student smelling of day-old cigarettes and mud.

I don't know how or when Tom found out I was Armenian. It seemed he'd always known. I remember his first question to me: "Are you a Dashnak or a Ramkavar?"

I had no idea what he was talking about. He repeated it. "Are you a Dashnak or a Ramkavar?"

What's that? I wondered. I was embarrassed that I didn't know what he was talking about. Was he asking me if I was Protestant or Catholic? Or was he referring to political parties? Years later, I would research Tom's words to find that Tom, a budding politician, had been referring to Armenian political parties.

Whenever I would pass Tom in the dorm or on the grassy quads between the cobbled stone buildings, he would flash his crooked grin and ask how his fellow "tribe member" was. Tribe, I thought proudly. Tom thinks I'm a member of his tribe.

Tom's first name was "Serge," an Armenian name he never used. I always called him "Serge," never Tom, a private nod to what connected us. It felt special to be the only member of Tom's tribe on this small campus. Special but weird. I felt shame that what bonded us was this shared heritage to which I felt little relation. Shame and embarrassment, like an imposter, proffered treasures she hadn't earned. Yet I flushed with pride every time Tom spoke with me. As a senior and student body president, Tom knew the ropes, teaching me early how to wrangle myself into classes designed for upper-class students only and how to take "incompletes" when you didn't want to finish a course. Not a good lesson to learn as a freshman. At one point, Tom said he had nine "incompletes" at once. How he graduated, I don't know.

Tom did graduate, though, and flew back to his Northern California roots to attend law school, another step on his way to the politician he would become. I stayed loosely in touch, sending occasional donations to fund his many political campaigns and reaching out whenever we were in Northern California. I was proud of Tom and what this member of my "tribe" had become. But that was the extent of our relationship.

———————

The day before the dream, I had written of my desire to integrate the Armenian soul within me with the American professional I had become. It felt like a far-off goal, something out in the future, something to strive for. Then Tom appeared to me in the middle of the night, not the scruffy, disheveled Tom of our college days or the pinstriped politician he had become, but a primal, healthy, muscled, strong Tom. A Tom I recognized but didn't recognize. I doubt that Tom, a city boy from near San Francisco, had ever held a hoe or tilled a field.

To understand the dream better, I imagined myself back in it and asked Tom why he had come to greet me. "To till the earth of your

Becoming, of our Becoming. To be strong and proud and full of light in our Armenian heritage." He wanted to acknowledge how far I'd come, embracing that part of him that represented the Armenian within me—the Armenian embracing the American, and the American embracing the Armenian. My delight in seeing him was my delight in seeing myself. I no longer had any shame or embarrassment about my heritage when I interacted with Tom in the dream, only love and de-light.

In the dream, I run into Tom unexpectedly, as I have run unex-pectedly into my Armenian self during the past few years. But I greet him with joy as I greet these deep, hidden spaces within myself. The journey is not easy, though, as evidenced by the sweat on Tom's brow. It's arduous, hard work and sometimes takes me to dark places, as most journeys of any significance do.

Tom stands firmly in the dream, his legs heavy in a wide triangular stance upon the soil he tills. He's masculine, representing my inner male who's happily doing the heavy work of excavating the long-bur-ied soul of my Armenian heritage while firmly grounded in the fertile soil. My feminine self greets Tom eagerly and with love, embracing the animus and ready to plant the seeds of integration at the center of the mandorla, the integration of the masculine with the feminine, and the Armenian with the American.

Finally, I believe that the dream serves as a guidepost, an affirma-tion of where I stand: the ground has been prepared, and soon the seeds will be planted. But I am nowhere near to collecting the bounty of the harvest. I may not be meant to see where the next part will take me. I can't guess what this field, and this journey, will ultimately yield. But I am grateful that Tom came to mark the way.

Chapter 26

Just Go Up:
Chavin de Huantar

*Caminante, no hay camino,
se hace camino al andar.*

*Traveler, there is no path,
you make the path as you go.*

~Antonio Machado

"Hurry. Hurry! We're going to miss the bus!" Jim was running ahead of me in the bustling Lima bus station, dragging our cumbersome bags behind him. The taxi scheduled to transport us from our hotel to the station had not arrived. Seeing our panic, the kind bellman sent his aging, toothless brother José to drive us instead. After circling the same block four times, it became clear that José had no idea how to get to the bus station, hidden amidst the Lima morning's beeping horns and rush hour traffic. After driving around for an hour, he finally dropped us off at a sign depicting pictures of buses.

Traffic screamed at us from every direction, and the flashing neon billboards advertising "Cusquena" and "Crown Plaza Lima" flashed in the early morning sun. Crowds of people crisscrossed the block-long station, zigzagging hurriedly from every direction. Commercial stalls advertising Hertz and Avis disrupted our path; men yelling "Taxi, taxi!" at the top of their lungs accosted us; and hotel hawkers rushed us at every turn. The blaring traffic outside contributed to the cacophony. I couldn't think straight and just followed Jim blindly.

Jim had never been late for a bus, train, plane, or deadline in his entire life, and I could sense his temperature rising. I desperately sought directions in my broken, rusty Spanish: "Por favor, dónde están los auto busses?" No one seemed to understand me. Finally, someone pointed to an escalator traveling down: "Alli." We ran down the escalator, bags bumping along after us, and sure enough, a row of buses appeared. An unfamiliar man waved us over, motioning us to follow him. Soon we were boarding the bus to Huaraz, the driver having been mysteriously alerted to wait for these lost and late gringos. This would never happen in the States, I thought.

Six hours and many winding roads later, we completed the 160-mile journey north and met our traveling group of seven, led by Jeffrey and Ciele, a couple from Iowa. The next morning we boarded another bus to the tiny hillside town of Chavin, located at ten thousand feet in the Ancash mountain range of Central Peru. Chavin is known for the Temple of Chavin de Huantar, a UNESCO World Heritage Site, and for the San Pedro cactuses that grow wild throughout its hills. Many historians consider the Chavin culture the oldest in Peru, and this temple the most sacred of early religious centers in South America. Pilgrims have long partaken of the brewed cactus as medicine to transport them to other realms and make connections to the divine.

On our first morning, we strolled the half-mile from our hotel to an exquisite swath of property owned by our local guide, Jack. Jack, a fit, slick, swaggering ex-pat American in his 50s, owned this beautiful property adjacent to the temple and hosted groups of travelers interested in the temple and drinking the San Pedro plant medicine, which he grew, harvested, and brewed.

Patches of the giant green cactus, eight to twelve feet high, peppered the property. Only a slender green chain-link fence and a gently flowing stream separated Jack's property from the temple complex. A pack of three snow-white llamas roamed the land, skittering away upon any human approach, their heads held high and eyes piercing us as if to say, "What the hell are you doing on our land?" Two-person thatched straw huts for sleeping bordered the property's perimeter, stacked high inside with llama and alpaca skins to use as comforters and ward off the evening chill. Blankets of little purple flowers nestled between the slim cactus stalks shooting high into the air. An aura of peace and serenity prevailed.

Jack and his young Peruvian compadres had constructed a labyrinth of small stones on one side of the property. At the hub of the maze sat a ring of seven two-foot black boulders meant to serve as stools. A lower stone in the center of the circular theater held a small white bone chalice carved with serpents around its perimeter.

On our first morning, Jack instructed us to line up outside the entrance of the labyrinth one by one and to move slowly toward the center, taking our seats on one of the seven stone stools. His Peruvian sidekick, Alvaro, thick black hair streaming down his long muscled back, stood beside the labyrinth fingering his Incan flute, a red beaded headband stretched across his temples. The lilting tones of the Andean melodies sang us through the maze, mixing with the cries of the lime-green parrots watching from the surrounding palm trees and the gentle gurgling of the river sliding over mounds of smooth boulders.

Reverence thickened the air as we each walked the labyrinth and took our seats. I felt I should bow before the opalescent chalice sitting like a treasured crown upon its black altar. That or laugh at the absurdity of the moment.

A thick green sludge, Jack's cactus brew, filled the chalice. Dirt clung to the cracks on the outside of the cup and ground into the serpents' skins. One by one, Jack poured an inch or two of the elixir from the chalice into a smaller vessel and handed it to each circle member to drink from. For the men, he filled the smaller cup to its brim. For the women, he poured less. I watched as each of us choked down the vile substance, which tasted and smelled like rotting algae. Some gagged, and others tried to keep from throwing up. At times, I turned away so as not to see their discomfort. With every pour, Jack encouraged the imbiber to drink more. Jack's attitude suggested that the more cactus we imbibed, the more worthy we might become of his admiration.

I alone said no. I wanted half an inch, no more. I resented Jack's pressuring us with his eyes and words, testing us to see how much medicine we'd dare to take, whether appropriate or not. Though a novice partaker of plant medicine, my one experience in the States had shown me my limits. I wanted no part of this macho drinking game.

When my turn came, I downed my half-inch of sludge, trying not to hurl, and then went and perched outside our straw hut, waiting for the medicine to kick in.

I have never been much of an aficionado of plant medicines, leaving Jim to make his yearly treks deep into the Amazonian jungle alone to commune with the plants and jungle shamans. But I'd heard that this particular blend of medicine was exceptionally gentle, so I had agreed to join this journey. I'd tried the San Pedro cactus once before in a Pasadena backyard and had had a significant experience, albeit accompanied by hours and hours of crippling nausea. I hoped that this journey might prove as compelling—sans the nausea.

———————

That first experience had occurred about a year before we landed in Chavin. A circle of thirty sat cross-legged in the backyard of an old Pasadena Victorian, less than ten miles from our home. One by one, we came forward as La Gringa, a South African curandera visiting from Cuzco, poured each of us a little cup of the medicine she'd carried with her from Peru.

After gulping mine and wanting solitude, I camped out on a mahogany window seat at the front of the house, waiting to see what would happen. For a long time, I felt nothing except the heightening nausea. Then suddenly, I felt my arms become very heavy, each extended upward and outward, perpendicular to the trunk of my body. My legs felt leaden and stretched down from the bench onto the hardwood floor, one foot crossed over the other. Suddenly I understood that my arms were stretched across a long, slender, wooden post running from the fingertips of my left hand to the fingertips of my right hand. Another long post held my legs, running the length of my body from six inches above my head down past my feet and intersecting the first wooden post behind my shoulders.

Suddenly, the image became clear.

Oh my God, I'm being crucified.

I felt no pain, but could sense my arms and legs attached to the wooden cross. I looked around the inner vision and saw two men hanging from crosses nearby, that common form of torture and execution in ancient times. Then the scene shifted, and I became the observer, watching the three men on the cross, none of whom I recognized. I felt no fear, only awe and curiosity, as a gentle tremor shook my body. I had the distinct sensation of being transported back to Biblical times.

Like in a dream, the locale shifted again. I became a man standing on a dusty dirt road, grit covering my open sandals. I silently watched a mob move down the street, yelling, gesturing, trying to get the attention of a long-haired, white caftan-draped man leading the way, a long-haired man who looked a lot like pictures one often sees of Jesus.

The scene changed again. I was in a white-washed, two-story wooden home, simple and ancient. More throngs crowded into the house, trying to move toward a particular guest, the young rabbi, Jesus. I watched, my heart quickening, incredulous to be there. I had become a witness to Jesus in his own time, watching him move through the streets and preach in people's homes.

I didn't know what to make of the experience. Had the San Pedro cactus, named after St. Peter, who holds the keys to heaven, transported me to the time of Jesus for a reason? To re-connect me to my origins and the origins of my people? Perhaps to return me to a place in my heart that knew this man Jesus and had always known him.

Soon after taking the San Pedro for the second time, I moved to sit in the stream bed, its gentle gurgling soothing as nausea began to kick in. Oh shit, I thought. Here we go again. I looked through the fence at the ancient temple, staring back at me from its hillside perch. The old temple had been constructed in 1200 BC, and the new one in 500 BC. The Chavin people used the temple as a religious center. Both temples were relatively intact, with 39 dark underground mazes and chambers. I had read that in ancient times, it was believed that young maidens had been sacrificed atop these temples, along with goats and llamas, to appease the Gods. In recent archeological excavations, sacrificial remains had been unearthed on the property.

As I sat beside the stream, the huge flat boulder next to me, large enough to fit a human body, became a sacrificial altar, its top worn smooth by the flowing water. I became the maiden, my head upon the glimmering black stone, awaiting the sword, one among many being sacrificed at the temple. I imagined a long line of ancient Indian and Peruvian women behind me, waiting to be led to the top of the temple to be sacrificed.

Then my mother became the sacrifice. And my grandmother. And a long line of my female ancestors stretching back in time.

I thought of my 15-year-old maternal grandmother married off to a man twice her age and left to care for his twelve brothers and numerous cousins. My silent, petite grandmother was always in the background, cleaning or cooking, or keeping the books at their grocery stores. At the same time, her jovial, illiterate husband, twice her size, entertained his family, his friends, and his employees with jokes and gales of laughter. I thought of my mother, that grandmother's daughter, also anxiously cooking, cleaning, primping, doing anything she could to win her husband's love, never sure if she succeeded, and never allowed to use her significant energy and intelligence to work outside the home.

I thought of how I, too, had sacrificed, carrying my mother's pain and the pain of her immigrant parents in my body, often lapsing into depression and overeating to cope with the unacknowledged feelings. I thought of how Memory herself had been sacrificed in my family so as not to remember a trauma that may have been too difficult to bear.

Was that what it meant to be an Armenian woman? To sacrifice for husband and family? I studied the faces of the female ancestors stretching back through the centuries, bowing their heads upon the stone of the sacrificial altar. A deep sadness overcame me, and I silently wept.

We all sacrifice, I thought, men and women alike, but there, that day by the stream at Chavin de Huantar, it was the sacrifice not only of the young Peruvian maidens but also the maidens of my Armenian lineage that lodged itself into my consciousness and stays there still.

———————

As the sun set on our little tribe that evening in Chavin, one of Jack's helpers lit a massive bonfire. We drank homemade quinoa soup and huddled in the 30-degree weather around the leaping flames as Alvaro played his flute. Jeffrey, one of our leaders from the U.S., still under the influence of the medicine, took off all but a pair of cotton shorts, his ribs jutting out from his thin, aging body. He walked the perimeter of the circle, hands in prayer position, bowing to unseen people. With his long flowing gray hair and near cadaverous body, he reminded me of a Hindu sadhu, a penitent begging for mercy. I sat shivering by the fire, watching the surreal scene: tall cacti surrounding us, fire roaring and licking the sky, and thatched huts awaiting our slumber.

What was I doing here? I asked myself. With nausea and the cold, I wanted nothing more than to return to my hotel room rather than sleep in the smelly grass hut. I eyed the makeshift outhouse, two long logs placed parallel over a bottomless dirt pit, and my heart sank, wondering how I would manage its rickety seating in the middle of the starless night.

What was the purpose of this journey? What had brought me here? Indeed, there was the fear of missing out on an adventure, but what else?

Perhaps I needed to come this far, to this land, to these cacti and this ancient temple to remind me of the sacrifices of my mother, grandmother, and female ancestors and to learn not to pass that particular sacrificial sword onto my daughter.

A day or two later, our little group piled into a van and drove for eight hours onto more winding mountain roads in Central Peru to reach the tiny hamlet of Yayno, ostensibly to experience another temple, this one ruined and crumbling, at the top of a densely forested hill. We arrived late at night and camped in the freezing thirteen-thousand-foot air on the side of a hill near the temple. I shivered in our tent and called Alicia back in California on my cell phone while the others laughed around the fire. I cried and told Alicia I didn't know what I was doing there. I wanted to go home.

The next morning, Jack once again poured his thick, green sludge for each of the men on the journey: David, Jeffrey, my husband Jim, himself, and Alvaro filling their cups to the brim. The women, including me, chose not to partake. After drinking the San Pedro and a quick breakfast, Jack and Alvaro led the way toward a path sloping gently downward and around an adjacent brown hill.

I had prepared myself for a little walk, not yet knowing where we were going or how long it would take. As we rounded the hillside, we suddenly came upon a single, cone-shaped mountain stretching a quarter of a mile into the sky, covered with dense, black foliage. Moss-covered boulders lay askew atop the hill, any sign of an actual edifice now long gone. Huge, flat, algae-covered vertical boulders buttressed the mountain's base, propping up the crumbling hill. I stared up at the mountain apex, wondering how on earth we would get there. I resisted the urge to turn and flee.

Meanwhile, Jack and Alvaro sauntered ahead, laughing raucously as Jim and Jeffrey, deep in the thrall of the plant medicine, inched their way behind us, stopping every five or ten feet to prostrate themselves upon the cold stones and commune with the earth. I urged Jim to get up. I couldn't understand why he lay, practically asleep, on the cold stones. I was torn between trying to keep up with Jack and Alvaro leading the way or staying and watching over Jim and Jeffrey. I had never seen Jim this way, stumbling a few feet, falling face down on the rock path, and not getting up. Every time he fell, I urged him to get up, to keep walking, and to keep up with Jack and Alvaro.

In our many years of traversing hills and mountains, Jim has always been the one up ahead, the proverbial hare to my tortoise, always the first to reach the summit and beckon me forward. I panicked, wondering what was the matter with them. Why weren't he and Jeffrey keeping up?

I skittered to catch up with Jack and Alvaro, fearing we would get lost in this rugged terrain if I lost sight of them.

"Which way does the path go?" I panted.

They looked at me and laughed. "Hell if we know," Jack said.

"Haven't you been here before?"

"Nope," they both responded.

Rage rose within me. These guys were supposed to be our guides, and they were as high as kites with no idea where we were going and no concern whatsoever for their charges lying flat on the earth behind them. They just pointed up to the top of the mountain as if to indicate, "We're going up there."

I lost sight of Jack and Alvaro as they disappeared into the dark moss of the mountain. I stared down at Ciele, Jim, and Jeffrey at the bottom of the hill, looking up, not knowing where to go.

Worried they might not find their way, I frantically yelled down to them, "Just go up. There is no fucking path."

I began to hack my way up through the dense brush, eyeing the heap of stones at the top. I watched Jim and Jeffrey to ensure they continued progressing up the steep incline. Finally, we all made it safely to the top, but that didn't abate my anger at Jack and Alvaro for their abdication of responsibility during the climb.

B ack in Chavin, on the last morning of our trip, we sat together in a small room on the first floor of our hotel, debriefing. Ciele asked each of us what the highlight of our two-week trip had been. While I have no memory of my answer that day, I will never forget hers.

"The highlight of my trip was hearing Jemela say, 'Just go up. There is no fucking path.' I found that so profound, like a mantra for how we should live our lives."

I stared at her incredulously. Ciele had misunderstood my anxious eruption on that mountain in Yayno for something other than what it was. She had seen it as a metaphor.

Now, years later, I do too.

When I am confused or uncertain where to go next, Jim will remind me, with a twinkle in his eye and a smile on his lips: "Just go up. There is no fucking path." And I will sit quietly in my meditation chair, close my eyes, and let the great Mystery that surrounds and nourishes me show me the way.

I will remember the images of Jesus preaching in the streets of Nazareth and the young maidens and my female ancestors prostrated on the sacrificial altar. I will remember from where I come and pray to whatever divinity that listens to continue to guide my journey up life's proverbial mountain.

Chapter 27

The Wedding Dance

Jim and I hurry to our seats at the white-draped, round table in the far rear corner of the crowded ballroom. We wade through dozens of tables with two-foot-high centerpieces of white roses, each seating at least ten people. Little plastic boxes of the traditional Jordan almonds given out at Armenian weddings sit atop each place setting. They promise the bride and groom health, wealth, longevity, and fertility. A tall order, I think to myself as I hustle past each table.

It's hard to hurry in the five-inch platform heels I've donned so I don't have to shorten the new purple chiffon dress for Em's "black tie only" wedding. I have to try valiantly not to trip over my drooping hem. I fuss with my rhinestone-studded purple shawl, artfully arranging it around my shoulders to hide my bare arms, trying to keep it from falling. Jim looks calm and unruffled in his dapper onyx tuxedo, a stark change from his usual attire of Levi 501 jeans, flannel shirts, and hiking boots.

Almost everyone in the rectangular space is already seated, including our daughter Alicia, awaiting the bride and groom's entrance. The band, too, sits waiting on the long stage at the front of the ballroom, a myriad of instruments resting on their laps; the square parquet dance floor lies empty in front of the stage. Tables fill every spare spot in front of and to either side of the stage and dance floor.

We're late, and I'm exasperated. I hadn't wanted to miss Em's entrance to her wedding reception. We'd taken a breather between the wedding on the hotel lawn in front of the ocean and the reception, retiring to our hotel room for a few minutes. And now we might miss her entrance.

As I finally reach the table and turn to take my seat, the African-American bandleader, with his chest-length dreads, motions to the ten other band members: black, brown, old, young, male, and female. Soon, the notes of an Armenian melody, their mournful cadences familiar to me from previous such weddings attended long ago, blast out from the front of the ballroom.

Wow, Em has chosen Armenian music to enter her wedding reception, I think, with great surprise. Em, my thirty-year-old niece, had been raised in American schools and churches, as I had. She's young and beautiful, a downtown Los Angeles fit model, tall and thin with long dancer's limbs.

Wow, I think again, my eyes beginning to tear at the sound of the familiar yet unfamiliar ancient cadences.

"Ladies and Gentlemen, please stand and welcome the bride and groom for the first time," booms the bandleader, stepping to the front edge of the massively long stage.

Before I can sit, 300-plus people stand to greet Em and her tall, handsome, fair-haired, and very American husband, Wade. Someone throws open the ballroom doors, and Em prances in, slender right arm held high above her head, clutching her bouquet of white roses, the other hand lifting the train of her sleeveless fitted designer silk gown. With her lithe figure and the close fit of her elegant dress, my eyes rivet upon her. A huge smile of joy lights up her dark eyes, and her long chestnut locks bounce around her bare shoulders.

This is one happy, relaxed bride, I think, remembering the nerves of my own wedding day and my desire to escape the reception as soon as possible to relax and get to the honeymoon.

Em drops her train and moves into the room, both slender arms held high. She glides into the center of the ballroom, with Wade right behind her. They dance opposite one another, alone in the center of the room, both hands held high in the air, gazing into each other's eyes, swaying from side to side, echoing each other's movements. Hmmm, I wonder, is this some ancient metaphor for marriage, this mirroring of each other's movements through the dance?

Soon, my oldest brother Bud and his half-Armenian wife Celeste join their daughter on the dance floor. Celeste holds a loaf of Armenian lavash bread in her hands and begins to break and sprinkle the bits over Em and Wade's shoulders. Later, I learn that this sprinkling of lavash is an ancient Armenian tradition designed to ward off evil spirits and promote happiness for the new couple. Wade's parents and the rest of the wedding party enter the dance floor. Celeste breaks into a big smile and links her pinkie with Wade's in the traditional form of this dance. Bud, grinning from ear to ear, links his pinkie with Celeste's.

"Please, everyone, join in the dance as we welcome Mr. and Mrs. Struiksma to their first dance as husband and wife," the bandleader calls out.

I sit and watch, smiling and enjoying the scene. as people from throughout the room stream to the dance floor. I feel too self-conscious about my minimal Armenian dance ability to join the throng. My heels, my too-long dress, and my flowing shawl only add to my insecurity. My right foot taps to the insistent beats of the music, nonetheless. I observe the older Armenian women negotiate the complex steps of the wedding dance, performing each step with the intention and grace that stems from having danced these dances their entire lives. The young American crowd joins enthusiastically, clueless but game to enter this unfamiliar spectacle.

Young and old, Armenian and non-Armenian, surge to the dance floor to join the line, one pinkie linking to another as the Armenian music beats its insistent cadence. The line lengthens and snakes around the floor, forming a spiral with Em, Wade, Wade's parents, Bud, Celeste, and the Armenian dance instructor, Tommy Bozigian, at its head and center. The spiral gets larger and larger and wider and wider until soon it occupies the entire dance floor.

I feel a lump in my throat and tears in my eyes. I'd forgotten how traditional Armenian weddings sometimes start with this ageless circle dance. While this lavish event overlooking the Pacific hardly qualifies as a traditional Armenian wedding, my niece has chosen a nod to her ancestral heritage by entering this very American ballroom in the heart of Laguna Beach with this Armenian circle dance.

I'd been introduced to the dance more than thirty-eight years earlier when I'd been a bridesmaid in Bud's wedding to Celeste. A few weeks before the wedding, Celeste had asked the wedding party to attend Armenian dance lessons in an old, dilapidated auditorium in downtown Glendale.

Armenian dance lessons? Why on earth do I have to take Armenian dance lessons? I thought with irritation. Still in my twenties, I felt overwhelmed with my graduate studies in psychology and my duties as an ESL teacher at a local university. This request just seemed like another task to be accomplished amidst the many on my already overwhelming to-do list. It also felt like an invitation from an alien world. I had never danced these steps, nor had I witnessed many of them at the previous Armenian weddings I had attended.

Tommy Bozigian, then in his early forties, had led the sizeable bridal party through the confusing, intricate steps. Hardly a dancer, I couldn't follow the steps and kept stepping on the toes of the bridesmaid next to me, clutching my pinkie to hers.

Tommy barked out the directions: "One step right, then circle your left foot forward around the right, two more steps right, one step left, raise your arms, then hop and stomp. Now to the left: one step left, circle your right foot around the left, two more steps left, then one step right, hop and stomp. Raise your arms as you stomp. Now two steps forward, two steps back, and twirl around. Now start the whole thing over again. Faster, now, faster." I don't remember how many dance lessons we had or even the Armenian dance at Bud and Celeste's wedding, but I sure remembered the dance now.

I recognize the compact, lithe, graying figure of Tommy Bozigian, now in his late seventies or early eighties, leading the crowd, clutching Em's pinkie at the center of the snaking spiral.

Then Elsie Pehlivanian, a regal Armenian woman in her sixties, similar in age to me, an opera singer who had taught Em and her two older sisters to sing when they were young, grabs my hand in one of hers. She nabs Alicia in her other hand and drags us onto the dance floor, ignoring our resistant pleas. We cut into the snaking line, and I find myself wedged between my handsome young nephews Jake, Matt, Chase, and Grif with their dark eyes, black tuxes, and close-shaved beards. We sidestep and kick, circle, and stomp, dragging each other from one side to the next in no discernible pattern, laughing so hard we can hardly speak. The line moves faster and faster as the music intensifies. We desperately try to follow the steps, but in the melee and at this speed, it's hard to know what to do.

"Watch that old guy in the middle," Grif says. "He seems to know what he's doing."

"That's Tommy Bozigian Grif," I shout. "He's the Armenian dance teacher—of course, he knows what he's doing."

"Raise your arms higher, Aunty Jemela, higher, like this," Jake instructs. For whatever reason, Jake, the youngest of my brother Jim's four sons, at 27, dances with a grace and competence unfamiliar to me among the male members of my family. He seems to follow these confusing steps effortlessly.

I, on the other hand, am trying desperately to stay upright in my ridiculous platform heels, heels that this chubby, 66-year-old woman has no business wearing. I strain to catch glimpses of Tommy's feet, trying to discern the correct order of the steps, but he keeps dancing out of view. I spot my brother Jim and his wife Cindy also gamely trying to follow the rapid-fire steps, raising their arms high in the air, pinkies connected, laughing so hard that tears are running down my brother's face. I cast desperate yet smiling glances at Alicia. Then I lose sight of her, lost somewhere in the belly of the snake.

The energy in the room shimmers electric as rows of the spiral bump into each other. No space remains on the dance floor. Laughter and energy radiate throughout the room.

No matter how hard I try, I can't keep the steps in my mind. Soon Grif, Matt, Chase, Jake, and I move in whatever direction the snaking spiral pulls us, making up the steps as we go. I try to relax into the music's staccato tones and the dance's rhythm. I dance like this for what seems like hours, but it is probably more like minutes. I see Jim watching, standing alone, hands clasped in front of him, an amused smile on his face. He rarely sees his wife and daughter dance at all, let alone dance in this frenzied, unfamiliar fashion. All our efforts to drag him out to join us fail. Jim plays the observer, as usual, taking in the scene from a distance. I'm just happy he's there.

"Ladies and gentlemen, please take your seats as dinner is served," booms the bandleader.

Breathless and flushed, I return to Jim and our seats as the servers bring the salad and Celeste introduces a pastor to recite the blessing before the meal.

Now that was an icebreaker, I think, still trying to catch my breath. What a great way to start a wedding reception with everyone on their feet dancing and laughing. Soon, Em and Wade float, hand in hand and glowing from the energy of the dance, to their long table at the rear of the ballroom, facing the band and the dance floor. They sit in the middle of the table, bright eyes lighting up their glistening faces, their souls still dancing.

The swelling in my heart matches the joy on Em's face as I begin to eat, complete with the experience of the familiar yet unfamiliar Armenian melodies, the whole room up dancing together, and my gorgeous nephews on either side. I sit in the center of this Armenian-American mandorla and cry inner tears of joy at this sense of coming home, after so many years, to this music, this dance, and these people I love so much.

Chapter 28

Shame

Sometimes I imagine myself back in Aintab, in Southern Turkey, on the Anatolian plain. I see myself in that town of the births of Armen and Yeranik and Jemela, my grandparents, and the city of my ancestors. It's 1895 or 1915, or somewhere in between. I wait, huddled, a wan, thin girl of nine or ten in the corner of my limestone home. My stockinged feet rest upon the colorful tree of life woven into the carpet, a family treasure adorning the hardwood floors, woven centuries before and passed down from one generation to another.

Large photographs of my great-grandparents and their parents in brown and sepia hang on the whitewashed walls. The mustachioed men sit stock straight and stare expressionless into the camera. The women in long, lace cotton gowns stand awkwardly alongside them, staring unsmilingly at the camera.

I sit, silently fingering the black obsidian worry beads stretched out upon my white-aproned lap. My mother scurries around the room, tidying things and trying to create an external order to calm the internal disorder she feels. We await a knock on the door or the sound of a loudspeaker from the town square. We have heard what has happened in other towns, the men being pulled from their homes and murdered en masse and the women driven at bayonet-point into the streets, dragging their toddlers and carrying their infants.

We have heard what happens these days to Armenians, and we live in fear, waiting.

Or maybe we live unaware as yet, happily going about our daily tasks, cooking pilaf over the open fire and tending the cucumbers growing in the garden. Perhaps we live isolated from the rest of the country and without communication, oblivious to what's transpiring in other regions.

If we knew, I wonder what that waiting, that dread of anticipation, was like. I wonder about the fear, the anxiety, and the feelings of helplessness.

I wonder about it all—the before, the during, and the after. I know a little about the after, but nothing about the before and the during. I don't know when my grandparents got out, or how, or what they knew and what they didn't know. I can only wonder.

I think now not so much about the actions and behaviors of the after, but of the internal feeling remnants stuck deep in their psyches.

I think about shame.

What must it feel like to have your husband, father, brother, and other men of the town, uncles, grandfathers, and family friends, pulled from their homes and shot, thrown into mass graves, or hung by ropes in the town square? What must it feel like to walk in long rows, driven from your home, without food, with few possessions, with the ever-present fear of starving to death or being shot? What must it feel like to know that a group of people not unlike yourself, your neighbors, are choosing to exterminate you, kill you and drive you from your homes?

All because of the suffix on your name, the features on your face, or the God you worship. Not for anything related to yourself, your personality, your behavior, or your accomplishments, but instead because of accidents of your birth and cultural heritage.

This is the nature of prejudice. I make you an Other because your skin is colored differently, your God has a different face, or your name has a particular spelling.

What must it be like to be treated as second-class, reviled citizens, unworthy of life? What do you carry within as a result of that? What do you pass, unknowingly, onto your children and your grandchildren? What kind of shame might you carry in your heart of being unwanted and vilified?

Certainly, to be Black, Latinx, or Queer in the United States is to understand this.

And for my family, to be Armenian in Turkey in the 20th century was to experience this.

Did they wonder, "What have I done? Who am I to deserve this?"

I think of my grandfather. How did he get out? How did he escape? What might his psyche have come to believe about himself that he was being run out of the land in which his family had lived for generations, for millennia? And having escaped, how might one adapt or not adapt to their new country? My grandparents and my parents after them chose to adapt, to try to fit in, so as not to stand out and be Other once again, as they were in the old country.

What do successive generations internalize about themselves and their meaning in the world? What led, on a deeper level, to my father changing his name and dropping the Armenian "ian" suffix, my mother dying her dark locks blonde and cropping her large Armenian nose to half its size? The expected behavior of an immigrant culture trying to assimilate into the larger whole? Or a way to cut the internalized shame out of one's being?

I think of Brené Brown's definition of shame as "an intensely painful feeling or experience of believing we are flawed and, therefore, unworthy of love and belonging." It's an emotion that affects all of us in some way and profoundly shapes the way we interact in the world. This shame arises when we look inward critically and evaluate ourselves harshly, often over things we have little control over.

I think about the myriad ways in which individuals respond to shame. Some shrink within themselves and their world, hiding. Others build emotional defenses, such as anger or denial, to shield the shame from themselves and others, trying to perfect their outer world to hide their inner one. Some project their shame onto others, hoping these others will shoulder the shame they cannot bear to carry themselves.

I don't know exactly how my mother or father might have felt about being Armenian. I only know the outward behavior of moving toward creating the perfect American life, a lovely home, well-behaved children, and successful careers. There was little time for, or value upon, self-reflection or introspection, let alone acknowledgment of feelings of shame or unworthiness. The shame, whether internalized or externalized, went unspoken. But at what cost?

I, their sensitive youngest child, felt it in my soul. I sometimes felt alone and disconnected from some of my family and my culture. I suspect that my grandparents, arriving with no money, no belongings, and neither skills nor language to fit into the new world, also felt disconnected. From their homeland, their history, and their families. And might they have passed, consciously or unconsciously, those feelings of disconnection onto their children and their grandchildren?

I believe that they may have.

Many times in my life, I have been ashamed of my Armenianness. My dark unruly curls, over-ample hips, and belly, all the ways in which I don't fit into the American norm, at least the American norm of my youth in the 1950s and 1960s in Southern California. We—and I—existed too largely, loudly, and darkly for this shiny sun-drenched world. And I felt shame. I sometimes still do.

———————

To the uninitiated, we Armenians look invisible, an invisible minority: Caucasian with white skin, dark eyes, and dark hair. If you've never met one of us, you will find little to distinguish us from other Caucasians. But if you look closer, you'll see a certain bulbosity to the nose, paleness to the skin, and melancholic, almond-like depth to the eyes. Our trauma may not show itself obviously and externally, but it exists nonetheless.

My grandparents may have carried this mantle of shame, of being cast out. What shame did my parents carry? What shame do my daughter and I carry? What causes someone to change their name and facial features, if not shame and a desire to fit in with the mores of the surrounding culture, and to not be treated as Other?

And what about healing? Where does healing come from? How do we heal shame and move beyond it? Can we heal a deep, internalized shame? How do we confront the Other within ourselves and embrace her?

We realize that we are not what our perpetrators did to us. We are not whatever they thought of us. What others do to us, say about us, and believe about us is not who we are. It is who they are. The healing comes from knowing who we are and where we have been.

I'm reminded of one of the lines from the worn copy of the Desiderata I have carried from one house to another, one room to another, for more than 40 years: "You are a child of the universe, no less than the trees and the stars. You have a right to be here."

Though cast out, exiled, and reviled, we all have a right to be here. We are all, in the words of theologian Henri Nouwen, *Beloved*:

Whenever you feel hurt, offended, or rejected, you must dare to say to your-self: "These feelings strong as they may be, are not telling me the truth about myself. The truth, even though I cannot feel it right now, is that I am the chosen child of God, precious in God's eyes, called the Beloved from all eternity, and held safe in an everlasting embrace."

I carry this paragraph from Henri Nouwen in my heart. It comforts me when I feel lost, lonely, and unworthy. It has helped heal the sharp sting of shame and reminds me that I, too, like my parents and grandparents and their parents and grandparents before them, have a right to be here.

Nowadays, when I feel shame's barbs reach deep into my heart, I remind myself to throw my shoulders back and stand taller. I think of the many-centuries history of my ancient forebears, of their will to survive in the face of one adversity after another, and all that they endured in order to create the life I now lead.

I cast out shame and remember where we have been, what we have suffered, and who we are.

On good days, I replace shame with pride.

Chapter 29

April 24ᵗʰ, 2021

"Each year on this day, we remember the lives of all those who died in the Ottoman-era Armenian genocide and recommit ourselves to preventing such an atrocity from ever again occurring," Mr. Biden said in a statement issued on the 106th anniversary of the beginning of a brutal campaign by the former Ottoman Empire that killed 1.5 million people. "And we remember so that we remain ever vigilant against the corrosive influence of hate in all its forms. We affirm the history. We do this not to cast blame but to ensure that what happened is never repeated."

~ *The New York Times*, April 24, 2021

It's Saturday morning on April 24ᵗʰ, 2021, the 106ᵗʰ anniversary commemorating the Armenian Genocide, a date that Armenians worldwide remember. Thousands, perhaps tens of thousands, march down Sunset Boulevard in Hollywood every year in solidarity, reminding us what befell our ancestors over a century before. President Biden, our 47ᵗʰ President of the United States, announced today that the atrocities at the hands of the Turks in 1915 constitute a genocide.

To many, this may seem inconsequential. Who cares whether the president of the United States acknowledges a genocide 106 years ago in a faraway country?

As I read the news on my newsfeed, texts and emails start pouring in from friends and colleagues far and near. Jim reaches me first: "Did you hear the news?"

"Yes," I reply, trying to gauge my reaction.

Growing up Armenian in the 60s and 70s in Southern California, no Armenian I knew doubted that my grandparents, and our ancestors, survived the genocide. It was never in question. It was a given and the reason my grandparents immigrated from Turkey in the first decades of the 20th century. Though never spoken of, it was as much a fact in my world as that I had brown eyes and curly dark hair. It just was.

Much later, when I began to work with Armenian clients in Glendale, I began to understand the great wound upon the Armenian diaspora of Turkey and the U.S.'s failure to acknowledge what happened to us in Turkey. A failure to recognize a solemn truth accepted by Armenians throughout the world.

To not acknowledge this truth, to act as if it didn't happen, creates a form of international gaslighting. To call a genocide a skirmish, a casualty of war, not the systematic, intentional extermination of an entire race, twists the truth in an almost incomprehensible way.

Previously, Presidents George W. Bush and Barack Obama had promised to acknowledge the genocide but failed to do so, fearing the wrath of Turkey, then a U.S. ally.

President Biden also promised. But he came through. This morning. One hundred-six years after the genocide.

Bryan Ardouny, the executive director of the Armenian Assembly of America, stated outright what many of us were thinking: "This is a really critical moment in the arc of history, in defense of human rights. The president is standing firmly against basically a century of denial."

At about the same time, Recep Erdogan, the prime minister of Turkey, towing the century-old Turkish party line, stated that Turkey would defend the truth against the lie of the so-called "Armenian Genocide."

What does it mean to acknowledge, to take responsibility for, an atrocity? Why is it important? The German government admitted it, took responsibility, and made reparations to the Jews for the Holocaust. But no such admission has ever arisen from the Turks, no taking of responsibility or accountability. Why does that matter? We Armenians are left feeling negated and crazy, as if what our ancestors witnessed and experienced never existed, like a wife who knows in her bones that her husband has been cheating. When he consistently denies it, she's left doubting herself and her sanity. Without knowledge, without truth, we cannot heal and move forward.

Today, my American president has acknowledged that my Armenian ancestors were the victims of genocide. Today my worlds overlap and join. My understanding of myself as an Armenian-American grandchild of genocide survivors and the acknowledgment of my American president meet one another inside the mandorla.

Chapter 30

My Mother, the Motherland

I sit coughing violently, as I have for weeks, sounding ever more like a dying seal begging for rescue. The fog outside my bedroom window descends on my brain, and my mind can't focus for more than a minute before another round of coughing disrupts it. My stomach churns with nausea. The cough syrup, DayQuil, Mucinex, and Advil designed to alleviate my discomfort only make my stomach roil more persistently.

I feel defeated. The little girl in the 66-year-old body wants to cry.

She wants her mother, someone to come to take care of her and tell her it will all be okay. But these days, Mom no longer lives nearby. She died four years ago. No more rushing over from the family home in Altadena, fifteen minutes away, no more arriving with Theraflu and vitamin C and Nana Chorba, the Armenian rice and yogurt version of chicken soup. No more sitting by my bedside, feeling my forehead to check for fever. No more clucking at me to not work so hard and to take better care of myself.

I could always count on Mom to come running when I was sick, even when I was in my 40s and she was in her 70s. She may have been busy the rest of the time, but she was right there when I was ill. Physical illness was a language Mom understood, having tended to Dad for decades through many life-threatening illnesses.

Though I could always count on Mom when I was sick, as a child, "Nuv," short for "Nevart," sometimes scared me. She could lash out verbally with seemingly no provocation whatsoever, leaving me frightened and baffled. One memory, in particular, stands out.

I remember four-year-old me discovering the dials on our old-fashioned, black rotary telephone for the first time. The phone rested on a kitchen counter, perfectly aligned with my four-year-old gaze. I gleefully lifted the Lucite receiver with my left hand and stuck the index finger of my right hand in one of the holes on the dial, winding the dial around and around and around, giggling all the while.

I had discovered a new toy.

Suddenly, Mom burst down the hallway into the kitchen from my father's study, eyes blazing, shaking her much larger index finger violently in the air as she ran toward me. "Jemela, stop that immediately! What are you doing? Don't you know I'm on the other phone talking with the plumber? You should know better!" She grabbed the phone piece from my little fist and slammed it back onto its base.

I stared, big-eyed and clueless. I had no idea what I had done. I had no idea what she was talking about, that she was conversing on the other extension in my father's study, or that the two phones were connected.

Shame overtook me as if I'd been discovered standing alone and naked, exposed.

As a result of Mom's unpredictable moods, I strove to mollify her and quell the waiting blonde lioness within her, which seemed everready to roar. Mom was a formidable force, and as a child, I often cowered before her. To defer a minute, to not "jump when she said jump," was to incur the wrath of the lioness. I feared this wrath and worked to keep her calm and purring at all times.

Whenever the lioness roared, I held myself accountable, as most children do. I'd sink into shame and guilt for whatever I had done and slink off to my little blue bedroom. I felt like I had been a bad girl. As a consequence, I tried harder to be "good." And every time she'd roar anew, I'd feel shocked, as if it were happening for the first time. I'd collapse again into tears and self-loathing and then go looking for the Oreos hidden on the top shelf of the pantry or the chocolate ice cream secreted away inside the basement freezer.

In many ways, Mom and I lived in different worlds.

Her favorite colors were sun yellow and chartreuse green, evidenced by the bright green polo shirts she paired with white Bermuda shorts in the summer and the yellow upholstery on the loveseats in our den, stark against the thick white shag carpet. The bright blonde of her bobbed hair and her easy smile radiated sunniness when not disturbed by something amiss, either internally or externally.

I, on the other hand, favored pale lavenders and pinks, light blue, and soft, melodious tones. I liked taking long, slow walks around the neighborhood, discussing the books I endlessly read, and emotionally connecting with whoever was around. On the other hand, Mom was a "doer" and a fabulous one at that, always working to improve her environment and everyone around her. I was happiest in bed with a book or talking for long hours into the night. Mom seemed most comfortable working around the house, cooking, and getting things done.

For the longest time, it was too painful to admit that my mother, who proclaimed to have a near-perfect life, may have been hurting. That something within her, rather than in me, troubled her. It seemed far easier to take the blame myself. That, at least, I could control.

Later, much later, after Dad had died and Mom was in her eighties, a different mother emerged. Relieved from the stress of caring for her sick husband and in the early grip of dementia, she became soft, funny, and loving, a mother who called me her "precious" and saw only the good in everything I did.

But also, for the first time in her life, she told stories of betrayal held long quiet within her. Tales of betrayal by the husband she adored, echoing perhaps other betrayals left muted within her by her father and uncles and maybe even brothers. My sister and I, her late-in-life confidantes, listened carefully.

But the betrayal she continued to silence remained the betrayal of the motherland. The motherland and its people who had cast out and rejected her parents. Though she personally never visited that motherland, its betrayal lived within her still.

There's a story in ancient mythology that I've always related to. When the ocean nymph Philyra gave birth to the half-man, half-beast Chiron, the mother abandoned her child out of shame and disgust at his ugliness. As a result, Chiron was left wounded and alone, essentially an orphan. He was taken in by the god Apollo, who fostered him and taught him the healing arts of medicine, herbs, gymnastics, archery, and music. From those teachings, Chiron became a great healer, healing others and himself. He became known for his skill in medicine, his wisdom, and his sense of justice, all qualities unusual in centaurs. Chiron learned to give to others that which he most needed. His original wounding served not as an impediment but as a source of motivation and inspiration, leading him toward compassion, insight, and achievement.

While hardly abandoned by my mother, our physical and emotional differences and my need for connection to something larger than myself and others led me to study philosophy, theology, and psychology. Like Chiron, I sought answers to the workings of the universe. Chiron exhibited compassion for the lonely, the cast out, and those yearning for love and meaning. Feeling a kinship with Chiron, the wounded healer, I became a clinical psychologist, trying to soothe the pain of others and to give the love and care I wanted for myself.

I don't know what motivated my father, the son of an immigrant shoemaker, to become a physician who helped bring children into this world. Perhaps he, too, had unconsciously heard the wounded Chiron's call. What wounds might he have been salving in his choice to bring new life into a world that once cast out his mother and father and murdered his ancestors? Perhaps he also served as my Apollo, modeling for me the wisdom and compassion of the healing professions.

My maternal grandfather, Hacop, whose mother was said to have burned in an Armenian church at the hands of the Turks, was known for his philanthropy and his sponsoring of immigrant Armenians to come to the U.S. Perhaps Chiron's call worked within him, too, motivating him to give his time and his resources to helping and healing others in ways that may have needed healing in himself.

And what about Mom, who studied to become a social worker in New York before marrying? She worked to help indigent children receive the resources they needed from the government. Her work may have echoed her own needs and the needs of the many orphaned Armenian children left behind after the genocide.

All conjecture, but I wonder.

———————

I also wonder, as I sit trying to quell my relentless coughing, what motivated the dreams and visions that came to visit me in the night in the months leading up to the Genocide Tour. They unnerved me, and I didn't know what to make of them. Were some unseen, unknown forces working within, trying to get my attention and awaken something of which I was unaware?

I had expected to love the ancient minarets and Grand Bazaars of my motherland, the land of my ancestors, finding the sense of home I had never experienced in Southern California. But what I witnessed there instead were visions of blood running down the Euphrates, women raped and starved on death marches, and villagers ripped out of their beds to be evacuated in the middle of the night. Whatever calls to prayer I heard failed to enchant me as they had in Pakistan. I found the floor-length veils and burqas covering the faces of the women oppressive and the limestone walls of my grandparents' birthplace drab and uninteresting. Rather than delight me, both the visions of the motherland and the motherland herself frightened me, much as my mother once had.

During the Genocide Tour, I came out of innocence about the realities of my ancestral homeland, just as I had once come out of innocence with Mom. I remembered the times I had refused to acknowledge truths about the darker sides of her character that I didn't want to face: the sudden outbursts, the frequent put-downs, the general unavailability. I had wanted to think it was all my fault, not hers. I had wanted to protect my vision of the good mother.

I came out of innocence about the realities of my ancestral homeland, but what of the complete silence in my family about our origins? Were the truths of the genocide too painful to bear, forcing them into the shadow of denial? Had the silence and the denial been necessary survival mechanisms for my parents and grandparents to move forward in the new world? Perhaps that had been the only way they could survive and build a new life.

How does one continue to love someone they feel has betrayed them? How does one continue to love one's mother, best friend, husband, and motherland after they betray us?

I wondered these things as I sat alone, trying to quiet my aching lungs and heal what physically ailed me.

The psychologist James Hillman has said that to experience real love and healing, we must first experience betrayal and then for-giveness. Only through forgiveness does real love become possible.

I had come out of innocence with Mom and, heeding Hillman and Chiron, accepted her imperfections and betrayals and loved her none-theless.

But can I forgive the Turks for their intentional and systematic slaughter of 1.5 million of my people and their unwillingness to take responsibility for this today? I'm unsure that I can or that many of my fellow Armenians can. If I cannot directly forgive the Turks for the genocide, then can I, as Hillman suggests, "ask or pray that their sins be forgiven?"

Taking Hillman to heart, I ask that someone, somewhere, some power greater and more enlightened than myself, send forgiveness to the Turks for what they have done. I call on the wisdom and compas-sion of Chiron to forgive the unforgivable.

As I sit in my chair coughing, I do not call anyone. I balance upright on my cushion, breathe deeply in and out slowly, relax my back against the wooden slats of the chair, soften my nauseated stomach, and let the pain in my aching head subside and drain down my spine. I continue breathing until my discomfort subsides and my heart fills.

I become my own good mother.

I work to heal the wounded healer within.

Chapter 31

In and Out of the Mandorla

Jim and I sit at our antique mahogany dining room table, inherited from Jim's grandmother when we married. I sit facing Bob, our pasty-faced contractor, his 60-year-old paunch protruding from his baggy blue jeans.

"Hey Je*Mela*," he says, mispronouncing my name, accenting the second rather than the first syllable. "What kinda name is that, Je*Mela*?"

I am not offended, knowing how difficult it is to pronounce my first name, and accustomed to this mispronunciation.

I stare at him for a moment, at his balding pate, contemplating my answer. It has been a question posed often to me throughout my life, in my world of Buds, Jims, Susans, and Lindas. My name translates into both Arabic and Turkish, but not Armenian. I can only assume that my namesake, Grandmother Jemela, was given a Turkish name due to her birth in Turkey. Neither is my last name, Macer, Armenian, since my father shortened his given birth name from Mahsereghian to the easier-to-spell-and-pronounce Macer.

"It was my grandmother's name. It's a family name," I tell him, purposefully not letting on the truth of my Armenian heritage.

"Oh, I thought it was German or something."

I glance at Jim, who watches me closely and says nothing.

Afterward, I question my behavior. Why have I not told Bob the answer beneath his question: "What is your ethnicity?" I knew exactly what he was getting at.

In these frequent interactions in my life, I am careful with disclosing my Armenian heritage. I am not proud of this. I gauge carefully what I project might be the response. Will the asker dislike and resent the Armenians like so many in my neighborhood, or will they embrace, welcome, and honor us?

I remember my embarrassment when my mother would bark loudly across the aisles in Armenian grocery stores, demanding to know if the stuffed grape leaves had sold out or why the string cheese had shot up in price. I had wanted to hide and disappear into the nearest black hole.

I recalled the physicians with whom I worked at the Glendale Adventist Medical Center, grousing about the constant complaints and aggressive demands made upon them by their Armenian patients. I remember the one physician saying, "None of us would ever talk with you if you had an 'ian' at the end of your name."

Bob had been goading me for weeks with his conservative sentiments, saying that Biden was ridiculous to wear masks during the coronavirus pandemic and referring to the Southern California beach town Santa Monica as "the People's Republic of Santa Monica," likening it to Mao Tse Tung's communist China.

Bob resides in a "red" town east of us, just north of Glendale, where over a million Armenians have relocated, effectively taking over the once-white, Anglo-Saxon town. I have heard for years the anti-Armenian sentiments from guys like Bob and don't want to go down that road. Bob does great work, always shows up on time, and has an eye for detail and foresight that promises to make our upcoming office addition proceed smoothly. I need him on my side and don't want to give him any ammunition that might derail our project.

When my friends Karen and Tom moved to the town where Bob lives, their realtor warned them about the Armenians and assured them that he would try to find them a house in a non-Armenian neighborhood. I had reddened with shame then but feel rage now in recollecting it.

Yet today, at the dining room table, with Bob, I chose my position outside of the mandorla, and though I feel some remorse about my response, if asked again, I would likely answer Bob the same way.

Armenian people exist all around me nowadays, walking with their elderly parents and young children in family groups around the neighborhood and working at the local TJ Maxx and flower shops. They call me "honey" and "dear" at the check-out counters as I purchase my sweet-smelling candles and soaps. I like being called their "honeys" and "dears," even though most look decades younger than me. I watch them closely. I smile at the difficult-to-pronounce names on their badges, their big brown eyes, and their wavy dark hair. I want to be with them, these members of my Armenian tribe, in my very American neighborhood. I no longer feel shame at their loud voices and hearty laughter. I recognize these attributes in myself. And I embrace them.

I'm often proud of my heritage and feel a deep-heart connection to my people. When our good friends and next-door neighbors, the Linkas, decided to move to Seattle in the middle of the pandemic, Catherine said, "We tried to find some nice people to buy our house for you." Catherine and Bob sold their home to a young Armenian family. I was thrilled, so happy to meet the young couple and their two children who now live next door.

I fantasized about inviting them over for stuffed peppers and grape leaves, roasted lamb, and baklava, just like the Sunday dinners of my youth with my extended Armenian family. I remembered the soft din of Turkish and Armenian spoken as background music by my elderly aunts and uncles and the old aunties pinching my cheeks and calling me "Yavrigas." I remember how the Armenian culture wrapped its warm cocoon around me without my knowledge, a welcome part of every week. Now, with my new neighbors, I welcome the possibility of recreating that and opening another portal into my culture, another entrance into the mandorla.

I realize I don't have any Armenian friends, having unconsciously migrated toward the blue-eyed blondes of my childhood, the Americans my parents sought to emulate. The one half-Armenian friend I had growing up died of a brain aneurysm years ago. Now, I am anxious to have more and to experience more moments within my culture.

My friend Kim asked the other day what countries rest on my travel bucket list now that the pandemic has subsided and international travel has resumed.

"Ireland and Bhutan," I answered quickly. It didn't enter my mind to mention visiting the present-day republic of Armenia. In my heart, though, I know it's near the top of the list. I have wanted to go to Armenia for a long time. My client Taline, my old country relatives, and others of my Armenian clients have all been. I have not.

A part of me fears the complete surround of Armenian people, many looking a lot like me, yet speaking a language I cannot understand and possibly living lives unlike mine. Jim and Alicia have little interest in Armenia. They would accompany me if I asked them, but I have a hunch this trip needs to be on my own or with my siblings. Taline tells me how beautiful the country is, how magical, and often sends me videos of Artsakh and Lake Sevan. But I fear I will feel alien, Other, not a part of. It's part of the mandorla I still need to step into. But soon, I tell myself. Soon.

I recently visited the street outside my old office in Glendale, relieved to see that the coffee shop Urartu, a fixture outside my window for 19 years, had survived the pandemic and stayed open. I warmly greeted the once-young Armenian couple who owned it. How uncomfortable and strange I felt entering the coffee shop years ago when I started working here. Surrounded by Armenians drinking espresso, talking loudly in a tongue I didn't understand, and reeking of clove cigarettes and Axe cologne, I had felt the stranger in my own land and went there rarely. This time, however, I felt at home in this gathering place named for the ancient kingdom of Armenia, and owned by immigrant Armenians from Iran, across from the office where I first met Taline and my other Armenian clients. The three of us, me and the owners, met in the middle of this coffee shop, Armenians in this American life, on a California street. I embraced them and ordered an Armenian coffee, thick, murky espresso laced with sugar.

Once repelled, now drawn. The complex teeter-tottering in and out of the center of the mandorla, in and out of the embrace of who I wholly am. I now feel and understand the deep connection to my ancient people, our land, and our faith. Mt. Ararat and all she represents reside deep within my soul. But still, in moments like the one with Bob, I falter and retreat.

I think about the issue of faith and recall the resonance I felt in Hagia Sofia, in the churches at Diyarbakir and Ani, and in the churches of my youth in Pasadena. I rarely read the Bible and no longer attend either the Presbyterian church of my childhood or the Episcopal one of my thirties and forties. But I recognize a faith structure deep in my soul that has always been there. I may not pray to Jesus, but I have always known him and feel peace wherever I encounter him. I recognize him as the prophet who guided my people, a prophet that gave them strength amidst adversity.

I personally pray to something less concrete than a person: an energy, a spirit, a felt sense of something greater than myself. But deep in my soul, I am also a Christian, borne of a Christian people, not in the sense of the evangelicals, the fundamentalists, or the far right, but in the sense of carrying and honoring a man that gave his life for his faith, much as my ancestors' lives were taken from them, in part because of their faith.

I think again of the funeral of my elderly cousin in that Armenian church in Studio City, where I heard the bearded priest chanting incomprehensibly in Armenian. It had been a wholly Armenian world, with barely one odar in the pews. I had felt both at home and foreign in that stark church, at moments within the mandorla and at others outside of it.

After this long journey, I appreciate what my grandparents may have experienced. I may have never heard it from their lips, but I now have a sense of their lives. I have visited their birthplaces and homes in ancient Armenia, and I carry their experiences within me. I have excavated a past I knew little about and taken within myself an ancient, battered culture that has survived against all odds and thrived here in the United States. I feel the long line of my ancestors on their ancient lands stretching behind me and know myself as a part of them. Once lost and cut off from me, my culture has been retrieved, not entirely, perhaps, but in a much deeper way than before.

I remember Grandma Jemela's exhortation to me ten years ago in a meadow on the side of the road in the Grand Canyon. "Heal me," she had said. "Live the life I could not live."

I look to the heavens and whisper to her again, "Have I lived the life you could not live? Have I succeeded?"

She nods and disappears.

I remember the meeting at the Mexican restaurant Mijares one exhausted Friday night with a colleague, who told me that a strange woman speaking in a language she didn't understand was whispering in her ear. "She says you should write a book. Are you writing a book?"

I knew then that it was my Grandmother Jemela whispering in her ear.

I seek her out again. "Is this what you wanted? Is this the book you wanted me to write?"

Jemela's mouth curls into a small half-smile, her eyes glisten, she nods again, and disappears.

This road has been long, stretching from far before the 1915 Armenian Genocide to this day. It will stretch longer down the road into the life of my daughter Alicia and the lives of her children and her children's children. They will carry the events of those ancient days in their bones and souls, as I do. My hope for them is the same hope I have for myself, that we will acknowledge our history and carry it willingly, knowingly, and proudly in our souls.

Epilogue

Several years after beginning this writing journey, I once again sit on Jim's treatment table as he lays out his mesa of healing stones on the living room table.

I choose the carved blue lapis eagle this time; the eagle is a symbol of vision and rising above.

I blow three strong breaths into the stone, asking that whatever is ready to be healed within me find its way into the stone. I hand the stone to Jim. He slowly unwinds my heart chakra and places the eagle over my heart. He again begins to circumambulate the massage table, gently rattling his small Peruvian rattle to calm the energy.

This time, as he journeys through the heart chakra into the lower world, he finds a single white skeleton slumped in the corner of the cave in the Cave of Wounds. The skeleton's right arm is raised and handcuffed to a peg higher on the cave walls. As in the initial soul retrieval six years ago, I recognize this skeleton as a victim of the genocide.

Then, in his mind's eye, Jim enters the Cave of Contracts. He finds a single red book, about 5 x 8 inches, sitting on a brown, rectangular coffee table. This time, he asks me to enter the cave on my own and see what the red book has to tell me.

I enter the cave tentatively and ask the red book what message it has for me.

"It has been a long journey, but you have come out the other side. You are safe now. Be not afraid."

I am touched by what the book has to tell me, and tears dampen my face.

Jim proceeds to enter the Cave of Gifts. In the cave, he finds an alligator. An alligator? This surprises me, having neither any relationship nor knowledge of alligators. I enter the cave, frightened by the alligator's rough, protruding scales and open mouth. I ask the alligator what gifts it brings me and why it is here.

"I am fierce. I am here to protect you. I will eat up anyone that harms you," he says. I laugh and take the fearsome, protective alligator into my being, glad to have its fierce presence within me.

Finally, Jim enters the Cave of Grace.

"There's a young, mustachioed man who looks to be in his twenties, wearing an olive green military uniform," he tells me. I blanch when I hear this, shocked at who has appeared. For I know who he is. I tremble as I enter the cave and ask why he is here today.

"I am the perpetrator, and you are the victim. We are One. Do not make me Other. I am a part of you, and you are a part of me."

My heart beats fast in this meeting with the enemy, this Turkish soldier who has asked to come to live within me. I know, though, that this may be true healing, knowing the enemy as oneself and oneself as the enemy.

I take him into my energetic field and became one with him.

Finally, Jim notices a regal eagle flying high above me, a spirit animal come to accompany me. I ask the eagle if I can fly with him. I climb upon his back, and we soar over Western Armenia. I look down on the scene of one hundred and six years ago, perpetrator fighting victim, victim fighting perpetrator.

We are all of the same piece. We are all one, different shadow sides of each other, different aspects of the mandorla meeting in the middle as one.

I thank the eagle for her vision and for flying with me, leading the way with winged Hermes not far behind.

Acknowledgments

First and foremost, I want to thank the small band of intrepid women who have been on this journey with me from the start. My colleagues in Pacifica Graduate Institute's 2018 memoir class, and our brilliant, loving guide, Jennifer Leigh Selig, Ph.D., read and re-read these vignettes, sharing their hearts and their wisdom.

I thank Lori Richards for her depth of knowledge and vision regarding craft and her poetic ability to see things in my work that I was unable to see for myself. I thank Karen Post for her astute photographic memory, attention to detail, grasp of the big picture, ongoing support, and for always pushing me deeper and further than I ever thought to go. I thank Peggy Cook for her constant emotional encouragement, deep friendship, and ever-ready ear and heart whenever I became frustrated. Her support and presence have been inestimable.

There are no words sufficient to thank Jennifer Leigh Selig, our memoir teacher and the publisher of *Between Two Worlds*. Her incredible work ethic, her passion for writing and teaching, and her knowledge of memoir have been awe-inspiring. Jennifer aptly titled this course "Writing Down the Soul," and her loving soul has guided me with faith and encouragement through every step of the writing, editing, and publishing process. Without Jennifer's structure and presence, this book would never have been born. What I have learned in these past five years about myself and the writing world ranks as one of the most significant experiences of my life.

Many friends have provided strength, insight, and support for me along the way. I thank Christy Claxton Brink for encouraging and even cajoling me into pressing "send" on the original memoir class registration in 2018 and for being a spiritual beacon in my life for many years. I thank Lindsay Bozzani for her deep friendship through fifty years and for her presence with me when we first encountered the many deceased souls from the Armenian Genocide. Her spiritual camaraderie has been a sustaining touchstone in my life.

Susan Picascia has been a soul friend walking this journey through life with me for many, many years, as has Deanna Bushman. I am deeply grateful for both of them. Ruth Salmon and Karen Basquez provided spiritual, psychological, and soul support during the final year of this writing. Catherine Linka provided a sane writer's perspective on this often daunting writing process. Susan Flynn offered early encouragement for this writing, and Jill Kelly edited the final manuscript with great attention to theme and detail.

Many Armenian clients have shared their lives and souls through my nearly forty years of practice as a psychologist. They taught me not only about our culture but about what it means to be an Armenian. This memoir could not have been written without them.

My four grandparents, Hagob and Yeranik Akullian and Jemela and Armen Mahsereghian, with their strength, resiliency, and quest for survival in leaving their ancestral homes and coming to the U.S. to escape the genocide in Turkey, provided the inspiration for this memoir.

My parents, Nuv and George Macer, through their hard work and diligence, created a life of comfort, support, and resources that enabled me to become all that I am. I am deeply grateful. Also, to my siblings, Lynne, Bud, and Jim, and their loving families for providing the ongoing, unspoken backbone of a large Armenian family.

Finally, I'd like to thank my husband, Jim, and daughter, Alicia, who walked with me with open hearts and generous spirits through this process. They suffered through endless discussions, helped with many panicked last-minute decisions, and provided much-needed encouragement too many times to count. Thank you, thank you, thank you for comprising my sacred little tribe in this life of ours.